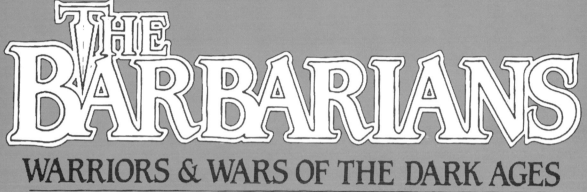

THE BARBARIANS

WARRIORS & WARS OF THE DARK AGES
TIM NEWARK

COLOUR ILLUSTRATIONS
BY ANGUS McBRIDE

BLANDFORD

For Lucy with Love

First published in the UK 1985 by Blandford Press
Villiers House, 41-47 Strand
London WC2N 5JE,
a Cassell Company.
Reprinted 1990

This paperback edition published in 1988

Distributed in the United States by
Sterling Publishing Co., Inc.,
387 Park Avenue South,
New York, NY 10016-8816

Distributed in Australia by
Capricorn Link (Australia) Pty Ltd.,
PO Box 665, Lane Cove, NSW 2066

British Library Cataloguing in Publication Data

Newark, Tim
    The barbarians—Warriors, weapons and
    warfare of the Dark Ages.
    1. Military art and science—Europe—
    History   2. Military history, Ancient
    3. Military history, Medieval
    I. Title
    355'.02'094   U43.E95

ISBN 0-7137-2042-5

Typeset by Graphicraft Typesetter Ltd., H.K.

Printed and bound in Hong Kong by Colorcraft Ltd.

Frontispiece

European man has always
feared raiding horse-archers
from the eastern plains. This
late 19th century illustration
emphasises the power of the
oriental composite bow.

Contents

Bronze horse-archers form the decoration for the top of an Etrusco-Campanian cauldron, c 500 BC, from the British Museum, London.

Preface

Barbarian was a derogatory name. An insult. The Greeks used the word for all those people living beyond their frontiers. It was in imitation of the foreigners' incomprehensible, ba-ba-babbling way of talking. Later, the Romans and their heirs, applied the word to European and Asian races living outside their empires who did not inhabit sophisticated urban settlements. These Barbarians were viewed as wild, savage people. From their archetypal appearance, the Latins derived their word for a beard, *barba*.

The general image we now have of the Barbarians is still very much one derived from Latin historians. Barbarians are seen as the antithesis of civilisation. Destroyers. For this reason, it has been said, our advanced societies must always be on their guard against Barbarian elements or lapses into Barbarism. This nightmare vision of the anarchic, savage warrior is represented by several dramatic 19th century illustrations reproduced throughout this book. It is an image that has persisted for over 2,000 years.

This century, however, has seen historical research begin to reveal a version of the Barbarian invasions in which the *status quo* of our civilisation was disturbed far less than has been supposed. The times were violent and much was destroyed, but essential power structures remained intact. The Barbarians simply adapted and adopted the systems they overran. Against that background, this book traces the means by which the Barbarians challenged the military might of a strong Mediterranean culture. It tells the story of a thousand years of armed competition.

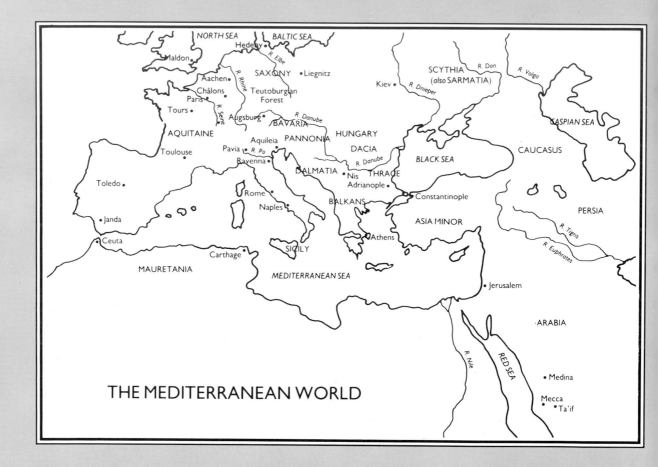

THE MEDITERRANEAN WORLD

The most terrible of all

THE HUNS
AND
EASTERN
GERMANS:
THE
4th TO 5th
CENTURIES

In AD 448, a group of ambassadors rode out from Constantinople on a mission to the land of the Huns. After 13 days, they reached Sofia. Over a dinner of lamb and beef, the members of the party discussed the merits of their leaders. The Romans praised their Emperor. The Huns exalted their King. Bigilas, a high-ranking interpreter, brought the argument to a head. 'Anyway, it is not fitting to compare a God with a man.' His Emperor being the God. The Huns were insulted. Tempers flared. Hands gripped hilts. Slowly, after gifts of Chinese silk and Indian jewels, the Huns were pacified. The mission would continue.

Reaching Nis, the devastation brought by the Barbarian raiders became clear. The city was deserted. Piles of human bones lay scattered by dogs and wolves. Passing that night amongst the ghosts, the ambassadors then rode on to the river Danube, the northern frontier of the eastern Roman Empire. They journeyed through rough, rocky terrain and lost their bearings. A servant cried out, the sun was not in the right place. Strange events were anticipated. On the banks of the Danube, the anxious became excited. Ferried across in primitive, hollowed-out logs, the Romans were now passing into alien territory. A few hours into the Barbaricum, the most important Huns rode ahead of the party to prepare their leader for the envoys. The next day, Barbarian guides brought the Romans to their King's encampment. The land in which this confrontation took place is now called Transylvania. The Barbarian King, for centuries afterwards, was represented in western portraits with dog's ears and goat's horns.

At first, the King of the Huns would not talk to the Romans. Only after sensitive negotiations were they led into his royal tent. The King sat on a simple wooden seat: no gilded throne. From his boots hung no precious beads: from his sleeves no little gold plates: on his head no sparkling diadem: no sword hung from his side. In contrast to the splendid Hun nobles that flanked him, the Barbarian King wore the plainest of clothes. This man was Attila. In later centuries, he was believed to be a monster. Today he is the most notorious of Barbarians. Such a reputation derives from failure.

Although highly successful in his initial command of the Huns, Attila never took his people into the Roman Empire to settle among the rich villa estates: the aim of all Barbarians. Attila never became absorbed in the Latin way of life. And yet, because of this life of raiding, he maintained an image as a barbaric outsider long after triumphant Germanic warlords had been accommodated within the Empire. Whether he would have become Romanised eventually is an open question, but dying as he did, in the wastes of the Barbaricum, he has remained the archetypal Barbarian. But what of his people? The Huns possess a notoriety to equal that of their master. And like Attila, their story is laced with tales of the supernatural.

Wild rumours reached the Romans in AD 376 of a new race of Barbarians. Witches expelled from amongst the Goths had coupled with the weird spirits that inhabit the wilderness beyond the Maeotic marshes to produce a savage people. Such tales were at first ignored by Romans familiar with fantastic reports from the Barbaricum. But then came news that the Germanic kingdom of the Ostrogoths had been shattered by a race of men never seen before. Sub-human, like centaurs, these warriors seemed indistinguishable from the beasts they rode. Their faces were hideous to behold; skulls deformed by binding when young and slits for eyes. Swollen cheeks disfigured by scars and covered in wispy hair. Soon the Visigoths were begging to be allowed within the Empire to escape the new horror from the steppes. Clearly the Romans had been wrong to doubt the existence of such a people. Churchmen, forever predicting the coming of the Antichrist, at last seemed vindicated. The Huns had arrived in Europe.

Swift in movement and ferocious in attack, the Huns must indeed have appeared to be the Horsemen of the Apocalypse. Of course, Europeans have always feared mounted raiders from the eastern plains. The Greeks wrote of horsemen from Scythia who devoured strangers and used their skulls as drinking cups. Germanic kings had to defend their Christian realms against pagan Avars and Magyars. While the Mongols very nearly made Europe a mere appendage of an Oriental empire. In the 20th century, this traditional sense of menace has been transferred from the horses and bows of Asian nomads to the 'eastern' tanks and missiles of Communist Russia. It is still the Huns, however, who remain the most terrible of all Barbarians.

Such dread was elaborated in the minds of victims and chroniclers. From the 4th century onwards, the Huns were demonised. To the Romans, the Huns were the most distant, and therefore the first and most ferocious people in a chain-reaction that hurtled Barbarian against Barbarian in the story of Imperial decline. The disintegration of the Empire meant the end of the world and so, for Christians, the Huns were the calamity that would precede the Second Coming. They were the forces of Gog and Magog: the Scourge of God. Reports of the alien Oriental features of the Huns contributed greatly to their fiercesome image. They were the stuff of nightmares and live on in folk tales as ogres covering vast distances in seven-league boots. Even the Avars, thought to be descendants of the

11

hordes of Attila, were believed to use magic to create illusionary effects in battle. Some opposing armies probably wavered under the pyschological impact of the Huns alone. Although much of this terror was in retrospect — the imagination of writers — and most professional warriors must have confronted the Huns with little regard for their reputation or alien appearance.

A great part of the success of the Huns lay in their prowess as horse-warriors. For as nomads, travelling across hundreds of miles of Eurasian steppe, horses had always been essential to them. And in order to control their herds of sheep and cattle, they had naturally developed horsemanship to a high standard. From these skills evolved the martial techniques of the Huns. Even the lasso became a deadly weapon. 'While the enemy are guarding against wounds from sword-thrusts,' recorded a Roman officer, Ammianus, 'the Huns throw strips of cloth plaited into nooses over their opponents so that they are entangled and unable to ride or walk.' The Huns spent so much of their life on horseback that they had difficulty walking. Like American cowboys, they developed a bowlegged gait. In battle, if ever dismounted, they considered themselves dead. Virtually every activity was conducted from horseback. Sometimes they sat side-saddle to carry out specific tasks. Negotiations with Roman diplomats were nearly always debated in the saddle. The horses the Huns rode were tough, shaggy ponies with short legs, common to the steppes. They were muscular and had great stamina. Their smallness gave the Huns considerable control over them and thus provided a stable base for archery as well as hand to hand fighting. Many of the stallions were gelded to make them easier to handle.

The excellent horsemanship of the Huns has often been ascribed to their use of stirrups. No such devices have been found that are attributable to the Huns. Instead, archaeological evidence indicates that stirrups originated in the Far East and only by the 7th century were in use in the Near East and eastern Europe. Besides, the Huns did not need stirrups. Their innate skill and small mounts gave them an advantage over most Western horsemen. The riding equipment of the Huns was primitive. They did not use spurs but urged their horses on with whips. Very few wooden saddles have been found and it must be assumed that the majority of Huns rode on simple stuffed leather pillows. To protect their legs from the sharp blades of long steppe grass, they wore goat-skin chaps.

When the Huns first burst into European history on the plains north of the Black Sea, they clashed with a group of steppe people called the Alans. Defeated, the Alans then allied themselves with the Huns and moved against the eastern Goths — the Ostrogoths — who in turn gave way before the invaders. History says that four hundred years earlier, the Goths had migrated from Sweden across eastern Europe eventually to settle in the grassland of Eurasia. The truth behind this epic journey has been questioned. The story is told by Jordanes in his 6th century Goth chronicle, but how could collective memory and oral history stretch back so far?

Hideous to behold, the Huns were 'demonised' from the 4th century onwards. This war trophy of a head hanging from the saddle was a practice originally ascribed to the Alans. From Guizot's *L'Histoire de France*, 1870.

Through its occurrence in other late Germanic chronicles, it seems that Scandinavia was a favoured home land in German folk-lore, whether true or not. For the northern lands were seen as strange and wild, and the home of so many mythical beings. It is possible, however, that the Goths did travel from the Baltic to southern Russia in much the same way as did the Swedes several hundred years later, sailing along the extensive waterways of Eurasia. Like the Swedish Vikings, the Goths were efficient sailors and their ships were already terrorising Black Sea ports by the 3rd century.

Living along the waterways of what the ancient Greeks had called Scythia, the eastern Germans became firmly established. They were no less fierce than the Sarmatian people they lived amongst. The Alans were reputed to wear the heads and flayed skins of their dead enemies on their horses as trophies. The Germans did not, however, fight in the same way as the oriental tribesmen who lived around them, and this may account for the shock defeats inflicted upon them by the Huns. Though adapting themselves partly to the bow and horse warfare of Eurasia, they strongly retained the instinct of their Germanic forefathers for fighting with spear and sword. They readily adopted the long lances of the Sarmatians but not their bows. The Ostrogoths probably also wore the heavy armour that was a characteristic of the Sarmatians. Made of overlapping scales of bone, horn and iron, it was sewn together with the sinews of horses or oxen. Some

Scenes from Scythian life. The upper drawing shows horsemanship typical of all Eurasian nomads. The lower drawing demonstrates the stringing of a bow as well as rudimentary medical measures. Both drawings are of friezes on electrum vases from the 3rd and 4th centuries BC, found in the steppeland just north of the Black Sea and now in the Hermitage, Leningrad.

14

armour was made from the hoofs of mares, split to resemble the scales of a dragon. 'Anyone who has not seen a dragon,' suggested the geographer Pausanias, 'is best advised to compare the appearance of a warrior clad in such armour to a green fir cone'.

The Sarmatians, an Iranian-speaking people, had dominated south-west Russia for several centuries but now, with the coming of the Huns, were in decline. It was among these tribes that the myth of the Amazons originated. Wearing men's clothes, long trousers and soft leather boots, Sarmatian wives were believed to join their husbands in hunting and battle. Virgins were not allowed to marry until they had killed an enemy in combat. Young girls had their right breasts scorched with a hot iron so that these might not prevent the girls using their right arms in fighting. Such stories are not without foundation. Ancient graves discovered in Russia have shown women lying next to spearheads, arrows and suits of scale armour.

The Huns were a wholly nomadic people. Driving their grazing herds before them, they trundled onwards with their families and felt-tents packed in huge wagons. Their origin is a mystery. Most often they have been identified with the Hsiung-nu Mongolians who terrorised the Chinese but were eventualy thrown back into central Asia. That these Mongolians then trekked across the whole of Asia seems a needlessly epic undertaking. They could have continued their activities much closer to home. Indeed, it was probably the Hsiung-nus switching of raids to peoples to the west of them, that then encouraged these people to move out of the Mongolian

Scythian archer on horseback, firing backwards. Greek bronze, c 500 BC, from the British Museum, London.

sphere of influence. Alternatively, it may have been a series of particularly devastating droughts – a regular hazard on the steppes – that broke the usual grazing cycles of tribesmen around the Aral and Caspian seas and spurred them on to new pastures, and thus clash with the Alans and Goths. On this basis, it seems likely that the Huns were an essentially Turkish confederation of tribes. A relatively open association, that no doubt also included tribes from further afield, like Mongolia. Such a force would have been totally horse-borne. It would also have been full of expert plunderers, for such a large unsettled group of people depended on raids and rustling to supplement its own drought-ravaged resources.

The Goth horsemen who first observed the relentless caravans of hostile, hungry people invading their territory must have been awestruck. To defend their homeland, they gathered together all able-bodied men in a roughly hewn army. The majority of these warriors were farmers and others engaged in settled pursuits. Unlike the professional raiders and marauders who comprised the armed retinues of their leading warriors and chieftains, these men did not own horses or swords, but fought on foot with anything to hand. When battle was joined, such men were hopelessly equipped to deal with the large numbers of Hun horse-archers. Refusing to engage in

A Eurasian horse-warrior clad in characteristic Sarmatian fashion. He wears scale armour and carries his lance in both hands, as did most horsemen of this period. This warrior appears on a marble stele found at Tanais, at the mouth of the River Don on the coast of the Sea of Azov. Now in the Hermitage, Leningrad.

16

close combat, the Huns preferred to pour a hail of arrows into the crowd of Goths. Howling and screaming, the Huns dashed about in wild bands, evading the charges of the lance-carrying Goth horse-warriors and then suddenly turning to pelt them with more arrows. Only when weakened and scattered by such attacks did the Huns then plunge amongst the enemy and swing sword against spear. These were the classic tactics of all true steppe warriors.

The bow the Huns used so effectively was the composite bow. The most deadly missile weapon in the Ancient and Medieval World, it was the primary weapon of all Oriental horsemen. It outdistanced the longbow and could penetrate armour at 100 yards/metres. So valued was it, that Hun nobles gave each other gilded bows as a sign of authority. The power of the composite bow derived from the combined strength of several materials. A wooden core was backed with layers of sinew and bellied on the inside with strips of horn. All these materials were then sandwiched together with an animal glue in a process which took much practice and was not easily mastered. The gluing of horn to wood was usually carried out in winter when cooler, humid conditions slowed — and thus toughened — the setting. Glue-soaked sinew was better applied on a warm spring day. The bow

17

would be left to set for two months at least. After its use, throughout the summer and autumn, it was unstrung and reconditioned. The combination of wood, sinew and horn produced a highly flexible bow which allowed a far longer draw than was usual from a short bow. It was thus ideal for use on horseback. Longer bows were more accurate, even if they became more susceptible to stress, but demanded a firm foothold and so were rarely used by horse-archers. The most powerful bows were stressed near to breaking point and needed to be warmed for an hour before being strung. Such easily-snapped bows were used for sport, while more sturdy and reliable bows were used in battle. Average range for use of a composite bow fired from horseback at the gallop was ten yards/metres. When standing still, a maximum effective range of 250 yards has been claimed. A major improvement in the design of the composite bow was devised in the Far East and Central Asia. The adding of strips of bone to the tips of the bow, holding the string, increased greatly its strength. This bone-reinforced bow was the weapon used by the Huns. Roman and German warriors highly prized any such bows picked up on the battlefield intact although they frequently lacked the expertise to use them effectively.

Gilt bronze belt plaque showing two wild horses fighting. Characteristic of Eurasian steppe culture, it comes from the Ordos region of China.

By AD 376 the Huns dominated Eurasia as far as the Danube. The Alans had been absorbed into the horde, while the Goths that had escaped asked permission of the Eastern Emperor to be allowed within the relative safety of the Empire. Such an entreaty was welcomed by the Emperor Valens as the Goths promised to fight with the Roman army. This influx of new recruits meant that money instead of conscripts could now be accepted from provincial landowners who preferred to part with gold rather than labourers. So enthusiastic were the Romans that they made boats available to ferry the refugees across the Danube. Roman officers escorted the Barbarians to ensure that they had disarmed as ordered. Such a condition of entry to the Empire was a severe blow to the Goth armoury, for their collection of weapons had been built up over years of manufacture, trade and plunder and could not easily be replaced. Valens even restricted Goth merchants to specific market towns where arms could not be bought. Fortunately for the Goths, most of the Romans escorting them were more interested in chasing good-looking women and picking up cheap slaves rather than enforcing the arms ban. Many Barbarian warriors slipped into Roman territory with their weapons hidden.

The shifting of a whole people is a massive operation. At one stage, rumours of the Huns being close at hand, sent the refugees into panic. Some desperately cut down trees, hollowed them out and tried to row across the rain swollen river. Many drowned. Once in the Balkans, the situation deteriorated. Corrupt Roman officials diverted supplies of food intended for the Goths and sold what little did reach them at highly inflated prices. Some Goths were reduced to offering their fellow tribesmen as slaves in exchange for dogs to eat. Famine and disease spread amongst the refugee camps. In their frustration, warriors began to ransack the surrounding countryside

and soon the Goths were in revolt. Marauding bands of Barbarian horsemen looted villas and ravaged the farmlands of Thrace. The consequences of the Hun migration were becoming dangerously clear.

On hearing this news, the Emperor Valens returned from the Near East in 378 with a veteran army and began to hunt down the freebooting Goths. Saracen horsemen with lances were sent out to harass the Barbarians. They were successful and brought back many heads. Next, the guerilla war was stepped up with a force of 2,000 picked troops installed in several walled cities. These Romans, carrying only swords and small, light shields, crept up on Goth gangs while they were foraging, resting, or drunk on their spoils, and efficiently butchered them. Such tactics slowly but surely curtailed the Barbarian raiding. Despite this, political rivals envious of the success of the task force commander, urged Valens to commit all his forces in one great battle to end the menace once and for all. Valens agreed and on the outskirts of Adrianople, receiving information that underestimated the strength of a nearby horde, he prepared for battle. He was advised to wait for the extra troops that his nephew Gratian, Emperor of the West, would soon bring. But impatient for military glory to equal that of this nephew, he ignored good counsel and left the security of his fortified camp.

It was a hot August day and approaching noon when Valens' legions spied the Goth encampment. In typical Barbarian fashion, the Goths had arranged their great four-wheeled wagons in a defensive laager. Within the wagon circle, the Goths yelled insults and war-cries as the Imperial army drew up into battle formation. Roman horsemen gathered on the right wing but those meant to secure the left flank of foot-soldiers were still scattered along the roads leading to the battlefield. Some Roman archers began to pelt the Barbarian wagons while legionaries clashed their shields. Anxiety began to spread amongst the Goths despite their initial ferocity, for a significant number of their horse-warriors were away foraging. Intermingled as they were with their women and children, their aggression must have been tempered with concern. Fritigern, the Goth chieftain, tried to buy time with proposals of peace. As envoys travelled backwards and forwards, his warriors started fires on the parched plain to increase the discomfort of legionaries already sweltering under the afternoon sun. For a group of Armenian auxiliaries the strain proved too much and they broke ranks, rushing against the Barbarian laager. The clash was short and hasty, and they were forced to withdraw ignominiously. The Romans considered it an ill omen.

The wait before battle must have been demoralising. Nerves, exhaustion and thirst would have stifled any remaining impetus amongst the lower Roman ranks to crush the raiders. Much of that day seems to have been spent waiting. Fritigern's delays were no doubt proving strenuous to both sides. Then, suddenly, all hell broke loose. The Goth horse-warriors had returned from plundering and now bore down on the weary Roman troops. Surprised and tired out, the Roman cavalry broke before the charging Barbarians and were soon joined by fellow foot-soldiers they had thus left exposed. With no massed ranks of shields and spears to discourage their horses, the Goths could dash among the disintegrating legions and use superior mobility and height to savage those on foot. Goths with lances rushed after fleeing legionaries as if pig-sticking. Those foot-soldiers who struck back suffered from the downward, crushing slashes of the Barbarians' long double-edged sword, the *spatha*. But this alone did not guarantee the Goth horse-warriors victory, for concerted spearmen can ensnare cavalry and determined swordsmen, with no fear of flailing hoofs, can cut and stab at both rider and mount. Chaos, however, had gripped the Romans and thrown their formations into a stampeding crowd. In the crush to escape the slaughter, soldiers were packed so closely that those who retained their weapons could hardly raise them. Many suffocated. Clouds of dust enshrouded the struggling, shrieking masses. Arrows struck from nowhere. Gangs of horse-warriors appeared suddenly to swoop murderously on isolated groups of legionaries. Those Goths waiting within the wagon defences now joined in the fury that threatened to engulf the Romans. Foot-soldiers with spears and clubs, anything to hand, slogged away at the Roman front and pushed it back. As escape proved increasingly remote, many legionaries returned to the offensive. In their desperation, in the crowd, Roman wounded Roman. The battle dragged on until exhaustion reduced all remaining resolve. Stimulated by victory, the Barbarians pressed forward across the heaps of dead and dying and pursued the routed Imperial forces. The Roman reserve of German cavalry had already disappeared. Emperor Valens was lost amongst his soldiers and killed in the chase that continued into the night.

Barely a third of the Imperial army escaped the disaster outside Adrianople. The Goths must have suffered heavy losses too but they had won a remarkable victory. On this battlefield, military historians have claimed that medieval warfare began. The supremacy of the horse-warrior had eclipsed the infantry-based tactics of the Mediterranean Ancient World. Such a neat formula is far from the truth. Before and after the 4th century, disciplined infantry could soundly defeat horse-borne armies. In 507 at Vouillé, Frank warriors on foot, wielding axes, broke a force of Goth cavalry armed with lance and sword, just like that above. Adrianople itself was not simply a clear-cut victory of Barbarian horsemen over legionary infantry. The Goth foot-soldiers that emerged from behind their wagons carried the weight of sheer hard fighting that capitalised on the surprise of their horsemen. Besides, the majority of Goths always fought on foot. The decisive factors against the Romans in this battle were the exhaustion of their troops, the shock of the returning Goths and then the ensuing chaos in which they could not offer an effective defence against the enemy, whether on foot or horseback. In addition, the Emperor Valens, by not waiting for extra military support, had proved himself an incompetent commander. The Roman army was not exclusively composed of foot-soldiers, and by the 4th century it included many fine horse-warriors, usually recruited from the Barbarians and frequently armed similarly to their adversaries. If the Roman cavalry at Adrianople had not panicked, they might well have proved equal, perhaps superior, to the Goths, as they did on many other occasions.

Free from Imperial restraint, the Goths rampaged through the Balkans. They attacked the city of Adrianople as the dead Emperor's treasure was believed to be hidden there. Apparently the Goths lacked the expertise in siege warfare to overcome the walls and met stiff resistance. To prevent the Barbarians from re-using the arrows fired at them, the citizens partly cut the cords securing the barbs to the shafts so that they remained in one piece in flight but on impact broke up. The Romans also used artillery mounted on the walls to great effect. One machine, called a 'scorpion' from the way its lethal catapult leapt into the air, flung a huge rock amongst the crowd of warriors recklessly charging forward. Though it crashed to the ground missing the enemy, it spread terror amongst the Barbarians. Beneath this storm of stone, javelins, and slabs of columns ripped from within the city, the Goths became discouraged and eventually withdrew. They continued to plunder the open country. Attacking only towns without walls or those given up to them by deserters. The Goths, however, could not resist the possibility of capturing Constantinople – capital of the Eastern Empire, with riches to exceed even those of Rome – and they rode optimistically towards this jewel. In this endeavour, the historian Ammianus claims they were joined by Huns and Alans.

Awe-inspiring in its wealth, Constantinople also presented a terrific bastion of walls and fortifications. Nevertheless, the Barbarians rushed forward with their scaling ladders and began the assault. They were assisted most probably by Roman prisoners and deserters who helped them to build siege machines. Amongst the Roman garrison, however, was a group of Saracen horsemen. Bursting out from the city gates, they engaged the Goths in fierce hand to hand fighting. The mad action of one Saracen so appalled the Barbarians that it passed into legend. Riding into the midst of the enemy, this Saracen with long hair and naked except for a loin-cloth, thrust his dagger wildly into a Goth. Howling terribly, he then leapt from his horse and bit the neck of the dying warrior, sucking the blood that flowed out. Shaken by this vampiric act, the determination of the Barbarians was further undermined by the sheer technical superiority of the defending Romans. The Goths left as swiftly as they had arrived.

To deal with the Goths, Theodosius, a renowned general, was called back from retirement in Spain. In the winter of 378, he arrived in the Balkans with an army probably similar to that slaughtered at Adrianople and inflicted defeat upon the Barbarians. Eventually, Theodosius was made Emperor of the East and concluded a peace treaty with the Visigoths which gave them substantial tracts of land within the Empire. Many were recruited into the army. Similarly, those Goths who had split from the forces of Fritigern after Adrianople, known as the Ostrogoths, advanced westwards into Pannonia and were accepted in peace by the Western Emperor Gratian. The Romans now hoped that the Goths would act as a buffer between them and the bulk of the Huns who dominated the Barbaricum north of the Danube.

After their initial inroad into eastern Europe, the Huns appear to have lost their impetus. Throughout the rest of Theodosius' long reign and into the first decades of the 5th century, the western Huns settled into a semi-nomadic existence. Raising their tents in Hungary, they were content to limit their movements to sporadic raids across the Danube. Factions grew amongst the Huns and they no longer acted as a unified force. Many were employed in Roman armies to defeat the invasions of German barbarians to the west of them. Others joined the gangs of bandits, deserters and refugees that continued to terrorise the Balkans. During this period, the Alans seceded from the horde and joined the Vandals in their surge towards Spain. A more cohesive and enterprising campaign was carried out by those Huns who remained north of the Black Sea. In the summer of 395, the eastern Huns tore through the passes of the Caucasus and broke into Persia and the Roman provinces of Asia Minor and Syria. They were rigorously defeated. Persian and Roman armies of horse-archers confronted them on equal terms and forced them back through the mountains. In that summer the Huns demonstrated the speed and range of their raids, descending as far as the Euphrates and Antioch.

By the middle of the 5th century, the robber bands of the Huns were welded once more into a single force strong enough to attempt an ambitious campaign. The western Huns were now led by two supreme chieftains — two kings — Bleda and his younger brother, Attila. Both these warriors began their reign by securing dominance over the northern tribes of

Bronze plaque in form of man. Thought to be Hunnic, though bearing Caucasian features, possibly Germanic. From the Ordos region, 1st century BC, now in the British Museum, London.

Sarmatia. From there, they glanced across the border towards an Empire that offered them more material riches than they could ever obtain in the Barbaricum. While a man could spend his whole life scraping a living in the forests and plains of Eurasia, any freebooter daring within the Empire could dress himself in gold cloth, eat bread and meat, have a hot bath, and get drunk whenever he wished. These were the prizes of civilisation!

In 441 the Huns violated a trade agreement by capturing a border market town. In justification of their act they claimed that the bishop of Margus had crossed the Danube and stolen treasure from Hun tombs. This was a frequent occurence, even amongst clergy. The Huns demanded the handing over of the bishop as well as any escaped prisoners harboured by the Romans. After several more frontier towns were devastated, the bishop agreed to his fate. But in the end he saved his own skin by promising Attila to betray the city of Margus. The bishop slipped back into his city, opened the gates, and allowed it to be annihilated. The season's raiding ended with a great gap rent in the Danube defences. The next year the Romans gained a respite through patching up a treaty. But in 443 they felt strong enough to defy the Huns' call for tribute money. Again Attila and Bleda invaded the borderland and this time they plunged into the interior. Town and country were wrecked as far as Constantinople where, outside the walls, the Huns were confronted by an army led by Romanised German generals. The Romans were beaten. The Emperor was forced to sue for peace and treble the annual tribute to 2,100 pounds of gold.

Within the horde, such success brought with it rivalry and in 445 Attila murdered Bleda and assumed absolute command of the Huns. To reinforce

Goth refugees crossing the Danube into the Roman Empire to escape from the Huns. From Guizot's *L'Histoire de France*, 1870.

his position he proclaimed that an ancient rusty sword, dug up and brought to him by a peasant, was the sword of Mars. He now had the approval of the God of War. Such a supernatural power seemed demonstrated when Attila launched a second, greater attack on the Eastern Empire in 447. Before the invasion, earthquakes shattered the land. Towns were swallowed up. The walls of Constantinople collapsed. Storms and plague followed. And then came Attila. The Romans decided to gather their forces together and meet the Huns in one final decisive conflict. They lost. Attila had broken the Balkans. But, that said, resistance must still have been strong enough to deter him and his people from settling there permanently, for they retreated back to Hungary laden with booty.

The victories of the Huns at this stage cannot be ascribed to the military superiority or inferiority of either side. Both forces fought with a similar armoury. Horse-archers supported by heavier armoured lancers formed the basis of most eastern European armies during this period. Advantage lay in numbers, morale and leadership, and this was frequently determined simply by the fortunes of war. In addition to these factors, the Romans suffered particularly from continuing economic crises and the draining demands of the Persian frontier. The Huns had little to lose and were driven on by the promise of plunder.

The composition of the Hun horde in this period was highly cosmopolitan. Warriors from all conquered races fought under Attila: Turks, Persians, Sarmatians, Germans and Romans. During his stay at the camp of Attila, envoy and chronicler Priscus was approached by a man dressed as a Hun nobleman. The man spoke Greek and revealed that he had been captured by the Huns in 441. He had fought well for his new masters against the Romans and been allowed to marry a Hun woman. He now dined with the leading warriors and led a life more prosperous than he had ever had as a Roman merchant constantly threatened by tax extortion and Imperial corruption. The number of horsemen fighting under Attila has often been fantastically exaggerated. Hordes of half a million have been claimed by chroniclers determined to make them seem overwhelming in order to excuse Roman defeats or glorify victories. Instead, it has been suggested what the average raiding force probably numbered about a thousand horse-warriors at the most. Attila's army would have been considerably large than this, but there again at any one time many contingents would have been engaged in separate plundering expeditions, like the Ostrogoths at Adrianople.

For three years Attila enjoyed the booty and tributes of the Eastern Empire, then, in 450, he turned his attention to the West. He proposed to march as an ally of the Western Emperor Valentinian and rid Roman landowners of the Visigoths that had settled in the south of France. By such a move, he intended to displace the Romano-Barbarian warlord Aetius as protector of the West and thus control Gaul and the Western Empire with the permission of the Emperor. A craving for plunder had been replaced by

Attila observes the savage battle of the Catalaunian Plains in northern France, AD 451. His demonic likeness is based on Renaissance woodcut portraits. From Ward Lock's *Illustrated History of the World*, 1885.

more sophisticated power politics. Attila seemed ready at last to leave his raiding and accommodate himself within the Empire. Relations with the Emperor soured, however, after Valentinian refused to give up his sister in marriage to Attila and with her half of his Empire.

In Gaul, dynastic struggles among the Franks saw one faction side with Aetius and the other with the Huns. When Attila crossed the Rhine, he faced a western coalition of Franks and Gallic tribes, Visigoths under Theoderic, and a Romano-German force led by Aetius. It was an uneasy alliance. Theoderic and Aetius had been bitter enemies for years. At first Theoderic was prepared only to defend his lands around Toulouse, but envoys from the Emperor managed to convince him of the need to present a combined front and save the whole of Gaul. As for Aetius, he had been a life-long friend of the Huns and fought with them on many occasions against Germans. Indeed, his use of the Huns to annihilate the Burgundians sparked off a tradition of epic poetry which culminated in the tale of the *Nibelungenlied*, preserving a Germanic dread of the Huns long after the event. In his youth, Aetius had spent much time with the Huns as an Imperial hostage and become a skilled archer and horseman. He knew their ways very well.

The two forces clashed in a titanic battle somewhere in Champagne called the Catalaunian Plains or *locus Mauriacus*. This is generally believed to have been near the town of Chalons-sur-Marne. Numerous peoples and tribes gathered here in June 451. Jordanes, Goth chronicler, wrote of the events of that day as if describing Armageddon. 'What just cause can be found for the encounter of so many nations,' he wondered, 'what hatred fired them all to

25

take arms against each other? It is evident that the human race lives for its kings. At the mad impulse of one mind, a slaughter of nations takes place. At the whim of a haughty ruler, that which nature has taken so long to create is destroyed in a moment.'

The battle began towards the end of the day. Horse-warriors rode from both sides to seize a ridge above the plain. Roman horse-archers clad in mail and scale armour dashed forward. Joined by Visigoth nobles and their retainers, wielding lance and sword, they captured one side. Along the other slope charged the Huns with allied German tribes. A great struggle now ensued for the crest of the hill. Archers let fly from afar while Germanic warriors thrust and hacked at each other. A contingent of Alans confronted the Huns, their former masters. Their loyalty was in doubt and so Aetius placed them between the Romans on the left wing and the Visigoths on the right. Now they could not so easily run away. Attila positioned his bravest and finest warriors in the centre, with Ostrogoths and other subject Germans on their flanks. As the fight for the hill intensified, foot-soldiers joined in. Those Franks allied with the Romans, hurled their famed tomahawk axes at the enemy before running into close combat. Other Germans, Romans, and Huns just battered away with spear and shield.

Eventually the Romans and Visigoths gained the upper hand and threw the Huns back down the hill. Attila rode amongst the action and rallied his men with words of strength. 'Let the wounded exact in vengeance the death of his foe,' he bellowed. 'Let those without wounds revel in the slaughter of the enemy! No spear shall harm those who are sure to live. And those who are sure to die-Fate overtakes anyway in peace!' Warriors hammered each other until exhaustion or pain overcame them. Theoderic, an old and venerable chieftain, encouraged his Visigoths against their kinsmen, the Ostrogoths. They fought furiously and in the crowd Theoderic was struck down dead. Angered by such a loss, the Visigoths pushed back their adversaries and fell upon the majority of the Huns. Many Huns and their allies now took flight while Attila and the body of his army retreated behind the bulky wagons of their encampment. As dusk drew on, fighting became confused in the half light, gradually ceasing as weary warriors made their way back to their camps. During the night, it was claimed, the ghosts of the fallen continued the battle.

The next day, each side awoke to the awful spectacle of a battlefield heaped with the slain and wounded. Slashed and cut warriors stumbled back to their tribal groups. If bound cleanly, their lacerations would heal. Those pierced by lance and arrow, bursting vital organs, stood little chance. Arrows with barbed heads ripped great holes in the skin. Those fired by the Huns were believed to be tipped with poison. Though this is probably not true, they most certainly did carry ordinary infection deep into the body. Inflammation and putrefaction set in and warriors groaned as sickness or disease claimed many still left alive after the shock of combat. Undeterred by the carnage, the Visigoths demanded to finish off the Huns. They burned to avenge their chieftain. Attila prepared for a last stand. Determined not to be taken alive, he piled saddles within his wagons to form a fire, upon which he would fling himself. But as the Visigoths grieved for their dead king and readied themselves for battle, Aetius consulted their leaders. He believed that with the Huns totally vanquished, the Visigoths, drunk with victory, would overrun the whole of Gaul. Therefore, he advised the son of Theoderic that others might sieze power in his homeland if he suffered badly in the forthcoming fight. Apparently accepting this counsel, the Visigoths left immediately for Toulouse. Aetius used a similar argument to recommend the withdrawal of the Franks. Attila and his mauled forces were thus allowed to retreat eastwards. It seems likely that Aetius wished to maintain the Huns as a force he could play against the Germans, as against the Burgundians. But he had made an error of judgment, for the Huns were not going to fade away until he needed them. Furious at his defeat, Attila and his horde rode into Italy.

From Aquileia to Milan, northern Italy was devastated. Such depredations only added to the famine and plague that already dominated the countryside. So that when news reached Attila of an attack on his territory by the Eastern Empire, he speedily returned to Hungary, sparing the rest of Italy. On the steppes of Eurasia, Attila planned a campaign against Constantinople that would ensure the tribute of the Romans forever. The opportunity never came. Celebrating the addition of another woman to his harem, Attila lay flat out drunk in his tent. He was not conscious of the nose bleed that ran down into his throat and choked him. In the power struggle that followed, the sons of Attila and the leaders of subject tribes tore the great Barbarian's kingdom apart. In a series of ferocious battles, the majority of the Huns were crushed by the Germans and fled back to the steppeland north of the Black Sea – the scene of their first victories eighty years before.

The Huns had ceased to be a threat to Europe and the Roman Empire, but the spirit of the Huns was not dead. Over the next few centuries, their infamy was absorbed by each new terror from the East. Although these were different confederations of tribes, led by other strong men, the West still called the steppe warriors Huns. Europe would not forget Attila. Despite their ferocity, however, and their damaging campaigns, the Huns did not destroy the Roman Empire. They had not even established themselves on Imperial territory. They were raiders not invaders. Like all other oriental nomads, before and after, they only scratched the surface of the European world. It was left to the German tribes to transform the Empire into great estates held by their warlords. The raids and invasions of the Germans grew in momentum over hundreds of years. From the 1st century to the 5th century. An assault not as dramatic as that of the Huns, but far more profound.

Fear in the forest

Six years after their slaughter by German tribesmen, the remains of governor Varus and three Roman legions – 15,000 men – lay scattered among the brushwood and bracken of the Teutoburgian Forest. Pausing in the middle of a retaliatory campaign across the Rhine, Germanicus and his legionaries solemnly surveyed the location of this disaster. It must have been a chilling series of discoveries: heaps of bleached bones and splintered weapons. On surrounding tree trunks the skulls of Roman prisoners had been nailed as a ferocious warning that Arminius, German chieftain, still dominated the forest. Survivors of the butchery pointed out the forest altars upon which captured tribunes and centurions had had their throats slit, in sacrifice to the northern gods of War.

Tacitus, the historian of this scene, felt that such a paying of respects served only to terrify even further Roman troops far away from their Gallic camps in the dank dark Teutoburger Wald. It is a tribute to the steady command of Germanicus that he managed to conduct the rest of his punitive expedition with some success. Fear can break an army. German warriors chanted on the battlefield before fighting. The tone of their shouts indicated whether they were terrifying their enemy or becoming scared themselves and thus foretold the outcome of combat. Some warriors held their shields in front of their mouths to amplify this noise. The Roman legions managed to reduce the natural fear of battle through uniform discipline and practised tactics. But in AD 9 in the western German forestland, such composure had given way.

Varus and his troops had crossed the Rhine and entered what they believed to be friendly territory on their way to putting down an uprising. This guarantee was given by Arminius, a young chieftain of the Cherusci, who had served with the Romans on several expeditions and been granted citizenship. Arminius, however, was a deceiver and wished to crush the governor Varus for hastily trying to impose Roman laws and taxes upon his people. Apparently reassured by Arminius, Varus dispersed many of this soldiers to assist in local village affairs while the main body of troops,

THE
WESTERN
GERMANS:
THE
1st TO 4th
CENTURIES

Germanicus buries the remains of the three Roman legions slaughtered by Arminius in AD 9. From Ward Lock's *Illustrated History of the World*, 1885.

wagons and camp followers trundled forward. Where secret forest paths proved insufficient, trees were felled and undergrowth cleared. Heavy rain fall made the ground slippery and treacherous. Ravines and marshland had to be bridged. As Varus advanced deeper into the dismal wood, Arminius excused himself from the main force and joined his gathering warriors. With the Roman soldiers scattered amongst wagons and pack animals, and bogged down in a sludge of roots and mud, the Cherusci attacked.

Howling and screaming, the Germans pounced upon the isolated groups of legionaries. At first, spears were hurled from the thickets. But then, as the Romans fell back in disarray, the tribesmen closed in and used the same spears as stabbing weapons. The dense forest and the shock of ambush prevented the Romans from assuming their battle formations and allowed the Germans to catch legionaries by themselves. In close combat, the physical presence of the Barbarians undoubtedly proved intimidating to those recruits from Mediterranean countries. Of a larger build, with an alien pale skin and red hair, the Germans frequently fought semi-naked, with chests adorned only with scars or tattoos, or wrapped in animal skins. Other wild sights confronted the Romans. Some young tribesmen, having let their hair and beards grow long so as to cover their face in accordance with a vow of manhood, now stood over a slain enemy and slashed at their hair. At last, through this blood of their foe, they had become worthy of their parents and homeland and could show their face. Exposed to such terrific attacks in a chaotic four-day running battle of relentless ambush, it is little wonder that few survivors of those original three legions emerged from the Teutoburgian Forest. Varus killed himself before capture by falling on his sword. His head was cut off and sent to Roman leaders south of the Rhine.

The Varian Disaster was a tremendous Barbarian victory over the Roman Empire and halted its expansion significantly. When news of the defeat reached Rome, soldiers had to be posted throughout the city to prevent a riot. Emperor Augustus and his subjects had been speaking of the recently explored land between the Rhine and the River Elbe as their latest province of Germania. Now all this was shattered, and Germany north of the Rhine never became part of the Roman Empire. Of course, the Romans could not leave this humiliation as it stood and over the next years conducted many retaliatory campaigns across the Rhine, not least of them the expedition of Germanicus. But essentially the German tribes remained unconquered.

The calamity of AD 9 was not the first the Germans had inflicted upon the Romans. 'Neither by the Samnites, the Carthaginians, Spain or Gaul, or even the Parthians,' remarks Tacitus, 'have we had more lessons taught us.' Earlier in the reign of Augustus, a legionary standard had been lost embarrassingly to raiders from across the middle Rhine. A hundred years before that, two roving German tribes, the Cimbri and Teutones, had threatened an invasion of Italy itself and defeated several Republican armies. But were the Germans superior as warriors to the neighbouring, defeated Celts of Gaul? With regard to military technology they were considerably inferior. For centuries, the Germans had imported finer iron weapons from the Celtic tribes of central Europe. The beautifully worked helmets and shields of the Celts were virtually unknown among the Germans; as was the Celtic use of chariots, which so impressed the Romans. Fortified earthworks like those of the Britons and Gauls were rare north of the Rhine. So why should the Celtic peoples of Spain, France, Britain and central Europe have fallen so completely to the Romans while conquest of the Germanic lands remained elusive?

Caesar's conquest of Gaul had succeeded partly because of dissension among the Celtic tribes. Many Gauls fought as auxiliaries with the Romans. Similarly, the invasion of Britain in AD 43 was undertaken because the Celtic Britons had become increasingly Romanised through their contact with Gaul. Invitations to intervene in their politics from factions amongst the Britons led Emperor Claudius to assume that here was a relatively easily-obtained feather in his cap. When the Celtic Britons did present a concerted opposition, as in the rebellion of Queen Boudicca, the Romans had a much tougher time.

In contrast to their southern neighbours, the Germans were not as familiar with the benefits of Imperial life. They lacked the sophisticated contacts that the Celts had with Mediterranean culture. They were less inclined to invite the intervention of the Romans. After all, it was their general hostility to the Romans over hundreds of years that maintained their cultural independence long after the Celts had become submerged in the Empire and lost their national identity. And yet, the Germans were tempted by the material wealth of the Empire and tapped it constantly through trading and raiding. In the end, it was the appeal of life within the Empire that spurred on the great invasions of later centuries. As for the fatal discord of the Celts, intertribal conflict was endemic among the Germans and many leading German chieftains sided with the Romans against their fellow countrymen. Opportunites were there to divide and conquer.

At this point, then, it must be remembered that the Romans had already conquered part of Germany. By 9 BC, Drusus, stepson of Augustus had conducted a series of successful campaigns beyond the Rhine and subdued the region as far as the River Elbe. Other Roman generals followed and all the main tribes had apparently submitted to Imperial rule. But this was

A late 19th century vision of the Teutoburger Wald as it would have looked when Governor Varus met his death there. In the foreground is an auroch, a species of wild cattle whose bulls, according to Caesar, grew to the size of elephants.

virgin territory. The slow process of Romanisation had only just begun when Arminius and his tribesmen threw out the remnants of Imperial occupation in the wake of the Varian Disaster. It was possible to defeat the Germans, but the problem was the maintenance of Roman rule. Strabo, a contemporary geographer, said that the Germans were like the Celts in every way, except that they were fiercer. This may have been true, although such a belief probably derived from the fact that the Germans were remoter and more primitive than the Celts. The decisive factor does seem to have been the guerilla warfare of Arminius. After such a calamitous defeat in AD 9, the Romans looked again at the strategic and logistical cost of re-invading Germany and decided it was simply not worth it. Gaul was near to Italy, a neighbouring land, whereas Germany vastly over-extended the supply routes of the Empire, and required a great investment of resources and troops. Besides, what was to be gained materially from colonisation of these inhospitable tracts of northern Europe? The Roman Empire was essentially a Mediterranean-centred economic community, and trade could always be conducted across the Rhine and Danube. And so, in the absence of any major weakness in the opposition of the Germans – such as existed among the Celtic Britons – the great rivers would provide a convenient natural frontier.

The victory of Arminius in the Teutoburgian Forest was won against all odds. The Roman army was superior in almost every way to its Barbarian

German warriors ambush Roman legionaries in the forests of western Germany. Guerilla warfare was the most successful opposition to Roman expansion in Northern Europe. From Ward Lock's *Illustrated History of the World*, 1885.

adversaries. The Romans frequently amazed their enemies with their advanced military technology. Caesar records the astonishment of the Gauls at Roman bridge-building, siege engines and warships. The Gallic chieftain Vercingetorix comforted his defeated warriors by concluding, 'The Romans have not conquered us through their courage in pitched battle, but with ingenuity. As in their knowledge of siege operations in which the Gauls have no experience.' Roman campaign management was overwhelming. There was a constant back up of food and weapons. The Germans, however, did not organise supply systems and relied on reaching enemy territory so that they could plunder for food. Every man took care of himself. Romans forewarned of a raid would stockpile all food in their area, so that Barbarians would be defeated by famine before battle was joined.

Even in close combat – the favoured test of arms and courage of the German warrior – the Romans possessed a superiority in weapons and armour. Germanicus encouraged his soldiers with a description of the military poverty of the enemy. 'The Germans wear neither breastplate nor helmet,' he claimed. 'Their shields are not even strengthened with metal or hide but are made of wickerwork, or thin, painted wood. They carry only spears and many of these are simply fire-hardened pointed sticks. Their bodies, while grim enough to behold, are powerful only for a short-lived onset and lack the stamina to bear a wound.' Certainly, in hand to hand fighting, the iron mail or plate armour of the Roman legionaries gave them a distinct advantage over near-naked Germans. The main weapon of the Germans was the spear, called *framea* by the Romans, and though this could be a primitive affair, many had short, narrow iron blades. These spears

Celtic bronze helmets from southern Germany, now in the State Prehistorical Collection, Munich. The Celts were far more sophisticated than their Germanic neighbours and possessed a superior military technology

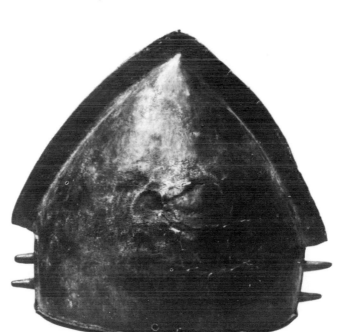

were either thrown or used in close combat as stabbing weapons. To this extent, spears had a longer reach than the Roman short sword and could have proved more useful for penetrating armour than a slashing sword. The Roman javelin, the *pilum*, could not be used as a thrusting weapon and this disadvantaged the Romans. Some historians refer to the Germans using 'long lances', by which they must mean pikes. Such long spears are most useful when the warriors carrying them maintain a strict close formation and present a phalanx of spear-heads. But there is no evidence that the Germans possessed the cohesion to carry out such tactics successfully and long spears would have proved unwieldy in guerilla warfare.

The German shield, so denigrated by Germanicus, was essentially a rounded wooden construction sometimes reinforced with an iron boss as much as 5 in. (12cm) long which could always be used as a punching weapon in the last resort. On most occasions, after having flung at the enemy the spears they had brought with them, German warriors depended upon picking up discarded weapons on the battlefield. When these proved scarce, they would fight with any rock or branch to hand. The battle-site

Celtic bronze swords from southern Germany, now in the State Prehistorical Collection, Munich. Many such weapons were imported or stolen by the Germans who then modelled their own arms after them.

Gallic horseman. Such warriors frequently fought as auxiliaries with the Romans. A proud engraving from Guizot's *L'Histoire de France*, 1870, showing how a 19th century nationalistic interest in the ancient glories of both France and Germany encouraged a Romantic image of the noble Barbarian.

after a victory was a treasure trove of weapons and many warriors must have combined Roman and Celtic arms with their native garb. Swords were rare amongst the Germans and, as they were expensive items, often imported, they would have been used by leading warriors only. Such swords as have been discovered fall into two distinct types. A short, single-edged sword or knife of native origin, and a double-edged thrusting sword like the Roman *gladius*. As the years passed and Roman contacts increased, Roman-style swords became widespread.

The majority of German warriors fought on foot as few tribes could bring large numbers of cavalry into the battlefield. The Batavi and the Tencteri were the only people noted for their horsemanship, the former serving as auxiliaries with the Romans. The growth of horsemanship amongst a people is partly determined by the landscape they inhabit. The plains of north Germany and the heathland, in areas where forest had been cleared for cultivation, no doubt encouraged mastery of the horse. Spurs and harnesses discovered in these locations reinforce this supposition. Cavalry in forests and marshland, however, is less effective and it seems that the subsistence living of most Germans did not encourage them to keep horses. Among these tribes, the few horses available became the preserve of chieftains and

Roman daggers of the 3rd century AD, now in the State Prehistorical Collection, Munich. Despite arms embargoes, these weapons found their way into Barbarian hands.

Silver decorated dagger belonging to a Roman officer of the 1st century AD, now in the State Prehistorical Collection, Munich. Roman daggers and short swords influenced Germanic weapon design.

thus denoted high status. The general standard of German horsemanship was thus not nearly as high as amongst the nomads of the steppes. German horsemen fought with spears, swords and shields, not bows, the supreme weapon of the horse-warrior. Indeed, archery appears to have fallen into neglect amongst Germans of the early Imperial period and was revived only in part in later centuries.

It seems likely that once German horsemen had ridden into battle, they preferred to fight on foot. Such a belief is fuelled by Caesar's account of a cavalry skirmish against Germans in which the enemy leapt from their mounts and began to stab at the Roman horses, thus bringing the riders down. Frequently, fleet-footed warriors accompanied groups of horsemen into battle, so it is unlikely that the horsemen acted as highly manoeuvrable cavalry contingents independent of foot-soldiers. In addition, the Romans observed that indigenous German horses were of a low quality, and they often had to mount their auxiliaries on horses imported from Italy.

With such primitive military resources, it seems baffling that the Germans managed to provide any resistance to the Romans at all. In such circumstances, a leader can only hope to make the most of the fighting spirit of his warriors through guerilla tactics. Having served with the Romans, Arminius must have observed how easily legionaries in strict order could absorb the headlong rush of the Barbarians and then employ troops on their flanks, or cavalry, to cut down the impetuous warriors. The Germans depended very much on the initial shock of their running attack. If this first charge failed to break the Roman line, the Barbarians usually came off second best to superior weaponry and tactics. On some occasions, as Caesar noted about the Gauls, the Barbarians ran over such distances, sometimes even up hill, that when they reached the Romans, they were utterly exhausted. Arminius preserved the wild energy of his warriors and exploited their familiarity with the treacherous German terrain through relentless short, sharp ambushes which eventually wore down the opposition. In their struggle against Germanicus, the Germans constantly tried to force the Romans onto swampy ground where, according to Tacitus, the water affected the Romans' ability to balance their javelins for a throw. The Barbarians even went to the extent of diverting streams so as to flood the ground the Romans stood upon. When beaten back by Germanicus, some Germans sought protection up trees, though these were later shot down by mocking Roman archers.

An important aspect of guerilla warfare is the spreading of terror. Atrocities like that described by Tacitus in the Teutoburgian Forest, though terrible, instilled dread amongst those advancing through 'Indian territory'. Indeed, Tacitus reflected Roman outrage at these brutal acts by calling them *barbarae*: savage. At this stage, however, one must question how shocking such incidents would really have seemed to Romans regularly attuned to the cruelty of the arena. While on campaign, the Romans were not adverse to wholesale slaughter. Caesar's massacres of complete German tribes are

notorious. Still, Roman soldiers did not look upon the prospect of serving on the northern frontier with pleasure, as the individual ferocity of the German warrior was renowned.

Like most primitive people, German men expressed aggressive masculinity through their appearance. Skin-tight trousers, animal skins and rough cloaks created a wild image. Some warriors shaved parts of their head to increase the bizarreness of their looks. Others, like the Suebi, gathered their hair into a distinctive knot standing erect on the crown of the head. If not naturally red, hair would by dyed. Caesar once surprised a band of Germans as they were bathing in a river and dyeing their hair. Above all, however, Germans judged a man by his courage in battle. German warriors fought as much for the respect of their kinsmen as to defeat the enemy. This can, of course, be said of the Romans who equally valued individual bravery. But whereas the Romans rewarded valour with military decorations, for the Germans their daring determined their very social standing. The hardest and most feared warriors held positions of power amongst their people. Commanders achieved the respect of their men through example rather than the authority of their rank. It was a disgrace for a chief to be surpassed in courage by his followers. Generally, it was regarded weak and dismal to obtain slowly through labour what could be achieved immediately through the spilling of blood. Cowards were despised. Barred from religious ceremonies and tribal assemblies, many ended their shame by hanging themselves. To this extent, aside from a few ruling families, the German tribe was a hierarchy of hardmen. This explains the wedge-shaped battle groups mentioned by Tacitus and called *cunei* by the Romans. Later historians have described these almost as if they were a sophisticated tactical formation, but it seems more likely that they were simply groups or clans of warriors tied together by kinship, with the few bravest at the front, and the rest sloping away to the back according to their bloodlust. In an environment where leading warriors could idle away a day feasting while others worked the land, individual violence was regarded as the only way to betterment. Such was the motivation of the warrior on the battlefield.

Though the Germans together presented a threat to the Roman Empire, they were not a united people. On one occasion, Romans were even invited to watch one tribe annihilate a neighbouring people. 'More than 60,000 were killed and not by Roman swords,' Tacitus enthused. 'Long, I pray, may Barbarians persist, if not in loving us, at least in hating each other.' But this was the inter-tribal warfare that had always gone on and always would. During the Imperial period, some Germans received Roman assistance. It was Imperial policy to create buffer zones of friendly tribes, and envoys were sent with gifts to those chiefs the Romans thought susceptible to such advances. Many German chiefs accepted an alliance with Rome more as an opportunity to defeat rival tribes than out of any love for the Roman way of life. Even within a single tribe, loyalties could be split by the possibility of employing the Empire against an enemy.

Among the Cherusci, Arminius began a feud by abducting the daughter of another chieftain, Segestes. As Governor Varus advanced to his death in the Teutoburgian Forest, it was Segestes who continually warned him not to trust Arminius. Later, Segestes was forced to flee to the Romans as the majority of tribesmen stood by Arminius. In his escape, he kidnapped the wife of Arminius, who was with child. As Segestes urged Germanicus in his campaign against the Cherusci, Arminius railed furiously at the Romans, 'Before my sword, three legions, three generals have fallen. I wage war not with the help of treason nor against pregnant women, but in open day and against men who carry arms!' After having maintained the German tribes in coalition against Germanicus and compelled the Romans back across the Rhine, Arminius marched against Maroboduus, one of the few German chiefs to rival Arminius in influence and skills of military command. If Arminius and Maroboduus had united their peoples they could have taken the Germans deep into the Empire. Instead, Arminius inflicted a heavy defeat on Maroboduus who was forced to take refuge with the Romans. For Arminius, success proved his downfall. He was killed in AD 19 by his own warriors who feared a leader too powerful to control.

With the fall of Arminius and Maroboduus, the Romans enjoyed a respite from the northern Barbarians. But the Romans never stopped regarding the Germans as a primary military threat; and throughout the 1st century the greatest concentration of legions in the Empire were stationed along the Rhine frontier and the Danube. During the reign of Augustus, a mere 1,200 men at Lyons were deemed sufficient to control Gaul, whereas eight legions, approximately 40,000 men, guarded the Rhine. These armies were composed of regular troops (largely Roman citizens) and auxiliaries, recruited from German tribes allied to the Empire. The auxiliaries often fought with their own native weapons and under the command of German chieftains with Roman names. It was through these warriors that the Barbarisation of the Roman army over the next few centuries was to take place. In the short term, however, they could prove as much of a threat to the Romans as a useful ally.

In AD 69, Julius Civilis united the Batavi with independent German tribes in a mutiny against Roman authority under the pretext of supporting a particular Imperial faction. He was joined by a Gallic chieftain who proclaimed an Empire of the Gauls. Eventually the unlikely alliance of Gauls and Germans broke down. No doubt because the freedom the Germans most wanted was the liberty to plunder Gaul. Both forces were defeated. In response to this rebellion, auxiliary troops were removed from their areas of origin to far flung frontiers and their command transferred to Roman officers. This could only be a temporary measure. By the 2nd century, the scarcity of legionary recruits from Italy meant that the regular army as well as the auxiliaries were made up largely of provincial warriors.

Fortunately for the Empire, the 2nd century proved a relatively quiet period along the Rhine. Under the Emperor Domitian, the frontier linking

Fanciful illustration of an ancient Pict with body tattoos. Engraved by Theodor de Bry after a drawing by John White, from the 1590 edition of Thomas Harriot's *The New Found Land of Virginia*. The intention was to show that the British had once been as barbaric as the native Americans were believed to be in the 16th century.

T·B·J·

the Rhine to the Danube was advanced to incorporate the Black Forest and the Taunus mountains into its defences. The main threat to the Empire in the 2nd century came across the Danube in the form of eastern Germans, steppe warriors, and the Dacian tribes. Of the eastern Germans, the Marcomanni, the Quadi, and the Vandals were the most vociferous. Causing considerable havoc in the provinces of central Europe, these Germans crossed the Italian frontier and raided as far as Aquileia before being chased back across the Danube by Marcus Aurelius.

By the middle of the 3rd century, the northern Barbarians had coalesced into the various peoples that would eventually fragment the Empire and were carrying out audacious raids. The Franks overran the lower Rhine, obtaining firm footholds in Gaul. Saxons and other tribes from the Netherlands and Denmark, harried the coasts of England. Crossing the

German tribesmen of the first few centuries AD. From *Costumes of All Nations*, 1907, originally published between 1861 and 1890 by Braun und Schneider, Germany.

Rhine and the Danube, the Alamanni plunged into Italy. In the east, the Goths ravaged the Balkans and Asia Minor. All these incursions were either defeated or controlled by Roman forces, but the routes of a future, permanent invasion had very clearly been laid. To some extent, the Germans had changed since described by Tacitus two hundred years earlier. Many of the old tribes named by Tacitus had broken down and fused into larger groups. The Cherusci suffered from prolonged internal discord after the death of Arminius and eventually disintegrated. Similarly, the Chatti and other north-western tribes on the frontier dissolved, to be reborn along with the Cherusci in the confederation of the Franks. Several pressures brought about this transition: not least being Roman diplomacy. The Empire constantly tempted German chieftains with the luxuries and higher standards of living south of the Rhine. Some Germans acquiesced and settled down in Gallic Roman cities: others did not. The resulting strain between those factions urging collaboration and those maintaining resistance frequently led to fighting, and split many prominent tribes. Another development altering the structure of several German tribes, was a greater centralisation around a warrior elite.

The close proximity of the Empire inevitably touched the day to day life of the Germans. Tribesmen had always raided the Celts, a wealthier people, but with the Celts' Romanisation and the presence of the Romans themselves, this activity accelerated. Trade also increased. In return for the sophisticated, manufactured products of the Romans and Gauls, the Germans could offer animal skins and amber. But these were luxury items, gathered only in particular parts of Germany. More readily available commodities were cattle and, above all, slaves. Both items were easily gained through raiding and war, with slaves becoming the primary export of the Germans. Such trade led to an increase in intertribal conflict as tribes launched slaving wars on each other. The Roman appetite for slaves was insatiable. At first, the Germans had little use for slaves: after battle, warriors returned to work the land themselves. But as the income from raiding and trading increased, the chieftains and their best warriors devoted all their time to this activity, leaving the less effective warriors and women to continue the farm labour. These were later joined by slaves, not sold, but given a little patch of land and expected to hand over a portion of their crop to their masters. A two-tier system now evolved in which chieftains and their followers became professional warriors while weaker men, women and slaves were confined to farming.

A successful chieftain rewarded his followers – his retinue – with the spoils of war: horses, cattle, slaves, weapons and food. Land was not yet part of the pay-off. In this way, wealth became concentrated among a warrior elite and was not shared with the whole tribe. The more successful a chieftain, the greater the number of retainers he attracted. Soon, these groups of warriors loyal to one charismatic leader, began to displace the old war bands based around the clan and kinship. Now, only in a time of great crisis – if a whole people were in danger – would the entire tribe take to arms. But as full-scale invasions by the Romans ceased to be a threat, any fighting in the tribe was carried out by these gangs of professional warriors. Because of their increased wealth, a chieftain and his retainers could afford to ride a horse, wear armour and wield a sword, thus furthering their status as a martial elite. The special sword favoured by these horse-warriors was a long, two-edged slashing weapon – the *spatha* – ideally suited to fighting from horseback. This became increasingly widespread amongst both Barbarian and Roman soldiers in the the late Imperial period. If, as in some of the later migratory invasions of the Germans, the whole fighting force of a tribe was needed, the lesser, common warriors continued to fight on foot with spears or whatever came to hand. Because of the authority and professionalism of the elite warriors, more sophisticated tactics, manoeuvres, and discipline could be expected from the Germans. The northern Barbarians were no longer near-naked savages.

With the accumulation of wealth and military power in the hands of the most successful war leaders, their political influence increased. Sometimes, such power was in opposition to the desires of the rest of the tribe and wayward retinues were exiled. In other circumstances, a particularly strong warlord could subject the rest of this people to his control. Such a dictatorial centralisation of power occurred in the 1st century under Maroboduus who ruled the Marcomanni almost as effectively as a medieval king. It happened also under Arminius, though he was killed before he could become an absolute tyrant. These were prototypes for later developments. The growth of a powerful military class separate from the rest of the tribe, is clearly a forerunner of medieval feudalism and knighthood. Such a process, however, occurred only among the most advanced German societies, those nearest to the Roman frontier. These tribes had the greater opportunity to obtain the superiority of arms and wealth needed to maintain a martial elite and subjected lesser German tribes to their control. From this action, larger associations of tribes evolved around the most successful warlords to form the great tribal confederations of the 3rd and 4th centuries. It was these warlords and their retainers who spearheaded the Barbarian campaigns of the 5th century.

Business as usual

THE VISIGOTHS AND VANDALS: THE 5th CENTURY

'Most sacred Emperors,' appealed a man who felt sure he could save the Roman Empire. 'It must be admitted that wild Barbarian tribes, screaming everywhere, surround and threaten every stretch of our frontiers. These savages are sheltered by forests and snow-bound mountains. Some are nomads and protected by deserts and the blazing sun. Others, hidden amongst marshes and rivers, can not even be located and yet they shatter our peace and quiet with surprise attacks. Tribes of this kind must be assaulted with a variety of ingenious armed devices.' Addressing the Emperor Valens sometime between 367 and 369, the anonymous Latin writer went on to describe a series of weird and marvellous military machines. On one page he described a chariot pulled by *cataphractarii* — rider and horse clad in steel scale armour. Driven into battle at high speed, the chassis and axle were fitted with knives and very sharp scythes to slash the ham-strings of a fleeing enemy. Elsewhere in the treatise, powerful *ballistae* were outlined. One, the 'thunderbolt', was strong enough to throw an iron arrow across the width of the Danube. Another, was mounted on four wheels for ease of movement on the battlefield. A javelin designed with spikes around its neck had a dual purpose. For if it failed to impale an enemy, it would fall to the ground and act as a caltrop, sticking in his feet instead. Further on, the anonymous author suggested a pontoon bridge in which calf-skin bladders could be stitched together to form a platform for soldiers to cross, with hair mats laid on top to prevent a slippery surface. Finally, a huge warship was proposed, powered by oxen inside the hull, turning gears which turned paddles. Such a ship would crush all before it.

Some of the weapons in this treatise were not as fantastic as they might first seem. The *ballistae* were versions of equipment already in service. Both the pontoon bridge and the animal-powered paddle boat have been utilised and adapted in later centuries. That said, aside from the *ballistae*, none of the other devices were constructed, let alone used in warfare on the frontier. They remained the imaginative solutions of one Roman citizen sufficiently disturbed by the Barbarian incursions of the late 4th century to try and do something about them. If only the Emperors of the East and West would listen to him, he must have thought, then the Empire could be saved. But the Romans were not lacking in their military technology. The wars against the Barbarians in the 4th and 5th centuries were well fought by Roman forces, often better equipped and supplied than their adversaries. It was other factors – political, social and economic – in the maintenance of a vast association of countries and peoples that saw the Empire slip piece by piece from the control of the Romans. Some of these problems were mentioned in the anonymous treatise. The author criticised extortionate taxes ruining farmers in the provinces. He wished to root out corruption amongst tax-collectors, cut extravagant expenditure, and prevent the fraudulent debasement of the currency. Certainly the Empire was being weakened through mismanagement. But it was also, more to the point, changing its character.

Frequent Barbarian raids forced many towns to erect sturdy walls. In their haste and with little money to spare, pillars, monuments and tombstones were ripped up and incorporated into ring-walls linking massive buildings, such as a basilica or an amphitheatre, into their defences. Only the essential administrative and financial institutions could be thus protected and towns visibly shrank. Harassed by Barbarian bandits and

Scythed chariots, equipped with automatic whips to goad on the horse. From the 1552 edition of an anonymous 4th century treatise *De Rebus Bellicis*, in which the author proposed several fantastic machines with which to combat Barbarian marauders.

Scythed chariot driven by a horse clad in scale armour. Also from the 1552 edition of *De Rebus Bellicis*.

Four-wheeled ballista strong enough to hurl a bolt across the Danube. A screw device allows the aim of the machine to be raised or lowered. From the 1552 edition of *De Rebus Bellicis*.

tyrannical officials, those craftsmen, traders and small landholders who could not find security within town-walls, fled to the country estates of the great landlords. Here, fantastically wealthy landowners absorbed even more land from their frightened, powerless neighbours. Tenant farmers now surrendered their freedom, becoming serfs tied to the land, in return for the protection and prosperity of their landlords. Self-sufficient estates evolved around fortified villas. Private armies were raised by landlords to protect their stretch of the frontier. In the towns, citizens took to arms to defend themselves. The armies of the government had become independent forces, either living off the land or taking over towns. These forces traded, farmed and set up industries, creating their own state within a state. They defended their property against both Barbarian marauders and Imperial tax-collectors. Power rested in the hands of landlords and warlords and these were the men, in the 4th and 5th centuries, who stood against the Barbarians in order to save their own individual privilege and prosperity. The saving of the Empire as a whole was a mere ideal harboured by a few historically minded writers.

With decentralisation came Barbarisation. Barbarian troops had long been incorporated into Roman armies. At first, they were auxiliaries armed and disciplined as legionaries. Then they fought under the Imperial eagle as allied, federated forces, brandishing their own weapons and led by their own chieftains. Finally, provincial armies were composed almost totally of native troops defending their borderland against neighbouring Barbarians envious of their greater material wealth. The armies of the late Empire looked and fought like their enemies. In the 4th century, an Egyptian woman wrote apologising for non-payment of her taxes with the excuse that her son had 'gone away to the Barbarians'. By this she meant that her son had joined the regular Imperial army. Even in the most Barbarian-dependent days of the Empire, however, Roman infrastructure still meant that Imperial armies were better supplied with arms and provisions than those of their adversaries.

Successful Barbarian chieftains, fighting on behalf of the Romans, rose to great power within the Imperial hierarchy. They had Latin names, lived the life of Latin aristocracy and were frequently sponsored by Emperors as official 'Defenders of the Empire'. But they were still essentially Barbarian. The famous Aetius and Stilicho were both Germanic landowners supported by bands of Barbarian warriors. Even the most notorious Barbarian kings, such as Alaric and Theoderic, were open to accommodation with the Empire and propped up their part of the frontier against further incursions. It was more to their advantage, more profitable, to settle Imperial land in return for services rendered, and live as a Roman grandee, than destroy everything Imperial just because it was Roman. Trade, agriculture and industry could all be enjoyed by the Barbarian who grabbed his land and towns, settled it and then defended it against others. Indeed, Barbarians were not keen simply to *steal* the land. They had not risked their lives against other

Barbarians and government troops merely to set themselves up in a bandit refuge. They wished to be legitimate. They wanted security and the legal acknowledgement that they were entitled to land within the Empire. Only by working within the law could Germanic chieftains hope to exploit and pass on their estates without being harassed by government troops. Tracts of land taken by the government from private Roman landowners and granted to the Barbarians were the most prized form of payment for military services rendered. In addition, these allotments were tax free. A great

Late 19th century drawing of a tombstone from Mainz, featuring a Roman horse-warrior (probably a German auxiliary). He carries a long cavalry sword, *spatha*, and tramples down a barbarian. Many details have now been obscured on the original tombstone.

incentive for Barbarians to toe the Imperial line and settle down. Which is what many did. Tax evasion could not be absolute, and it was Theoderic who stressed to his Goth followers that though they need not pay anything on land given by the Empire, if they then invested in extra land they would be subject to the same taxes as the Romans. After all, Theoderic had as much to gain from efficient tax collection as any Imperial magnate. Wrangles over deeds of settlement and taxation fuelled much of the conflict between Empire and Barbarian throughout the invasions of the 5th century and later.

'Invasion' is itself an overestimation of several Barbarian movements within the Empire. Frequently, Barbarian confederations were allowed or invited on to Imperial territory. That said, in many regions of the Empire groups of Barbarian raiders did find themselves to be the dominant force and took control of activities in these areas through violence and intimidation. These invasions increased in their magnitude as Imperial authority retreated, until warlords had absolute command of huge stretches of land. In such circumstances, Roman legality and attention to correct tax assessment could go to hell! When the last Roman Emperor of the West was deposed in 476, it was not a sudden cataclysm but acknowledgement of the established fact that the Empire had been broken up into independent estates ruled by Germanic warlords. It was dangerous to pretend otherwise.

Claims to the Imperial title could lead to civil war, as in the past, which would prevent Barbarian chieftains from enjoying their newly-acquired wealth. The Germans wanted peace and security as much as anyone, but on their terms. This then is the 'Fall of the Roman Empire'. As Abbé Galliani wrote in 1744, 'Empires being neither up nor down, do not fall. They change their appearance.' The Germans were not just vandalic raiders. They wished to transform the Roman into a German Empire, or more properly, into an assembly of Germanic kingdoms. In this they succeeded. Power was handed from Roman landlords to German landlords.

With these concerns in mind, Barbarian migrations throughout the Empire were not so much raging floods of anarchy as ambitious quests for position and possession within the Roman system. Of course, military power had to be demonstrated and towns, especially on the frontier, were devastated. But German chieftains realised that to destroy the very fabric of the Empire was to reduce it to the impoverished conditions of the Barbaricum, which they had thankfully left far behind. Such a view did not always agree with the desires of their warriors. On the banks of the Danube in 376, Goths swore to smash the Empire in revenge for the sufferings they had endured from the Romans before being allowed within the frontier. In the years following they savaged substantial areas of the Balkans. The Romans, however, frequently achieved in peace and subterfuge what they failed in war. After Adrianople, the Emperor Theodosius made increasingly attractive overtures to the Barbarian leaders. They were invited to sumptuous feasts within the walls of Constantinople. Goth chieftains saw for themselves all the wondrous goods that flowed into this city. Spices and silk from the Far East: grain and oil from Africa: gold and silver from all round the Mediterranean. The full panoply of the Imperial army paraded before them. Clad in mail and scale armour from head to foot, Roman horse-warriors carried banners in the shape of dragons which twisted and hissed in the wind. 'The Emperor is God on earth,' exclaimed one excited Goth, 'anyone who raises a hand against him commits suicide.'

Laden with Imperial gifts, many Goth chieftains returned to their warriors and urged them to forget their Barbaric oaths of destruction. Instead, they should work with the Empire and relish a higher standard of living. Not surprisingly, the rank and file warriors were less than happy with this compromise, as it was their chieftains who benefited most while the rest came off second best to the Roman citizens with whom they were supposed to share their land. Tensions grew. With their chieftains ensconced in the luxury of Constantinople, many Goth warriors and their families were put to work on the farms of Roman landowners. They had become slaves while their rulers advanced up the Imperial ladder. Rebellions broke out. Goths joined with Roman peasants in an attempt to overthrow the state. But Goth chieftains, now risen to high office in the Roman army, rode out and crushed the rebels – once fellow tribesmen, now merely wretched slaves spoiling the status quo.

Barbarians on the move. The classic vision of whole tribes migrating into the Roman Empire. From Guizot's *L'Histoire de France*, 1870.

51

Dwelling within the palatial apartments of the Imperial capital, it was hard for Barbarian nobles to resist the internal politics of the Empire. Byzantine factions depended on the muscle the Germans could bring to their machinations. Stilicho, a Vandal by birth, enjoyed the patronage of Theodosius and became his leading general. Unfortunately, on the death of Theodosius, Stilicho was in Italy installing one of the dead man's sons as Emperor of the West. The other son shakily assumed the Imperial diadem in the East. Stilicho's rivals took advantage of his absence and one of them, Alaric, broke away from the Roman army and rampaged through Greece. Surrounded at first by a retinue of Romanised Goth warriors, he was joined by those Barbarians and peasants who saw their only salvation in the looting of villas and sacking of towns. In AD 395, this robber army elected Alaric, King of the Visigoths. Whether they were all true Visigoths is unlikely but it gave them a legitimate facade for their activities. The warriors that presented Alaric with this title were in no mood for compromise with the Empire. Regardless of any notions he may have had of strengthening his position within the Imperial hierarchy through a display of violence, his men roamed westward in search of plunder. They clashed several times unsuccessfully with Italian forces led by Stilicho and for a decade their advance faltered and lingered in present-day Yugoslavia.

The Visigoths that followed Alaric were largely a gange of marauders, which constantly changed as it overran new estates and absorbed the peasants and armed retinues of Roman landlords. It was forces such as these that carried out the more adventurous of the Barbarian migrations of the 5th century. A picture of hundreds of thousands of Barbarian families – wives, children and parents – moving as a whole to new lands does not ring true. Only in Gaul, where the Franks, Vandals and Burgundians had control of the borderlands, is it acceptable that their people should then cross the frontier and follow their warriors into land vacated by the Romans. After all, the population of Gaul was not enormous and its farmland had for a long time proved attractive. In this way, the Franks increasingly won – and settled permanently – large districts of northern Gaul. But those Barbarians, like the Vandals and Goths, who journeyed far through Italy, Spain and Africa, must have long left their native people behind. Only a few unrelated camp followers can have rumbled along with them in their wagons. Most of these wagons being full of arms, booty and valuable prisoners, with perhaps only the families of the ruling chieftains in tow. The majority of wariors took their women and wealth from the land they were given by their lords or granted by the Romans. Besides, a number of the warriors fighting with the Barbarians at any one time were likely to be disaffected local men; tenants bonded to their land and now taking revenge against their masters; runaway slaves and bandits seeking better opportunities for outlawry.

All such wild elements within the Barbarian horde had to be kept well under control. For though their fury was useful in battle, they could prove

Eight hundred years before the sack by Alaric, the Celtic Gauls sacked Rome in 390 BC. The Capitol held out for seven months. According to legend the citizens of the Capitol were alerted to a Celtic night attack by the honking of the sacred geese of Juno. A late 19th century engraving, from a painting by Henry Motte.

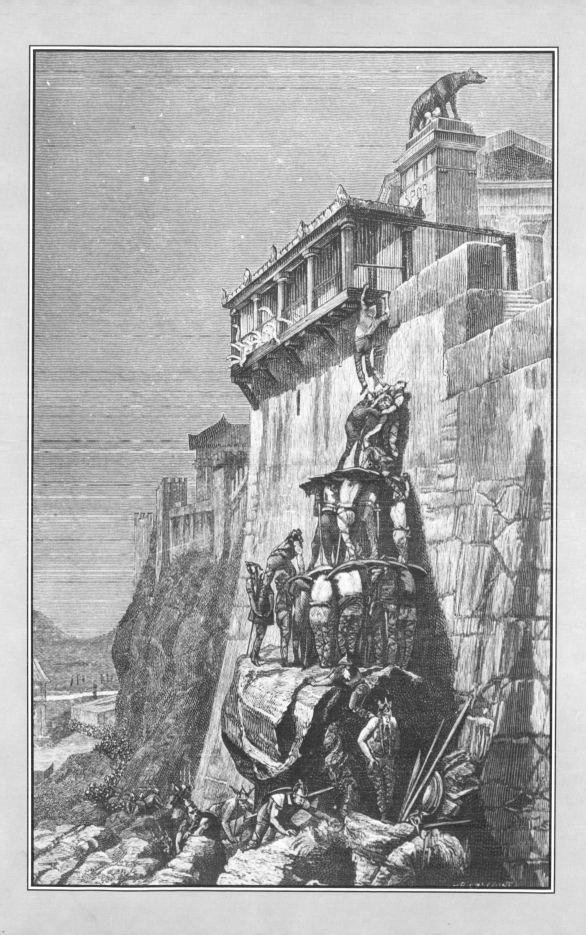

Fragment of mail showing rivets securing each ring. Late 6th or early 7th century, from Sutton Hoo, Suffolk, now in the British Museum, London.

a handicap to negotiations with Imperial authorities when a chieftain eventually wanted to set himself up in a provincial landholding. This conflict of interests, one which had fractured the Goths in the Balkans, proved a constant problem to Alaric and an annoyance to his men. In addition, a string of defeats by Stilicho had badly shaken his leadership. So that the treaty finally agreed with Stilicho, in which Alaric received an Imperial subsidy to defend his province against other Barbarians, seemed like the last straw to many adherents. These now rode off to join a horde of Germans streaming through the Alps. Stilicho had got the better of Alaric, neutralising him just when Italy was at its most threatened. He could now deal with the latest Barbarian raiders without having to worry about the Visigoths. But just when Alaric was beginning to settle down with his Imperial pension in Dalmatia, news reached him of Stilicho's assassination in 408. The opportunity for an almost unopposed advance into Italy proved too great. Alaric snatched it and rode into central Italy towards Rome. What little Imperial defence remained was centred around Ravenna, the newly established capital of the Western Empire, safe behind the marshes of the Po delta. Rome, the very symbol and heart of the Empire, had been left exposed.

As Alaric and his followers approached the great city, the magnitude of their endeavour suddenly struck them. Rome had not seen an enemy within its walls since Celts from Gaul had assailed it in 390 BC. For eight centuries the Imperial capital had been the storehouse of a vast treasure collected from its Mediterranean provinces. It was the most glittering city: the centre of the Empire: the centre of the world. Powerful politicians, multi-millionaire merchants, all lived within its walls, decorating their own palaces as well as creating some of the most remarkable and famous buildings in the Ancient World. In the 4th century, the city's walls had been renewed and raised. This does not seem to have filled the Emperor Honorious with much confidence. For it was he who moved the political, if not the spiritual capital of the Western Empire, to Ravenna. With him travelled many of Rome's richest citizens, thus denuding the city of part of its moveable wealth. Still, enough of the splendour and legend of Rome remained to inspire awe in those Goths riding towards it. A thunderstorm gathered over the surrounding countryside. Many Goths felt that the old Classical Gods had not deserted their home. One warrior proclaimed that he saw, 'Thunderbolts hurled against us. Divine fire flickered in front of the walls. Heaven, or was it Rome herself, raged in the storm.' But there was no need to worry. The Barbarians would not have to do battle with the Gods. Mortal treachery opened the gates of Rome without a struggle.

When Alaric entered Rome in AD 410, centuries of preserved treasures greeted the gaze of his warriors. According to chroniclers, Alaric allowed his troops to loot the city but not destroy it. He risked his leadership and life if he denied his men the rewards of pillage, their only payment, but he does seem to have wished to save the structure of the city. Perhaps he envisaged it as his own capital. Or perhaps he wished to make peace with the Emperor and this was a sign of his good intentions. Perhaps the city was just too vast and its buildings too well built for him to bother with their destruction. Jordanes, Christian Goth apologist, suggests that Alaric restrained the excesses of his wild men so as to protect churches and holy places. But, though a Christian, Alaric was an Arian. A member of a heretic faith that believed in the divinity of God the Father but not of Christ. Like other Arian Germans, he did not have much respect for Catholic shrines. Indeed, in later years, there were bitter religious wars between Arians and Catholics, with the latter only emerging triumphant by a narrow margin. For Roman Christians, the arrival of the Visigoths was as bad as that of any pagans. Fortunately for them, Alaric and his followers did not relish their occupation of Rome for long. They moved southwards after only a few months: their chief concern being food. Italian towns, especially Rome, depended heavily on grain and oil shipments from Africa and these had been stopped once news of the Barbarian invasion had reached Romans there. Food supply had always been a weak point in the campaigns of the Barbarians, and now there was no food even to plunder. The Visigoths were forced to ride southwards, and planned to sail to Sicily and then Africa. But as they prepared for their voyage, Alaric died. The great chieftain was buried with all his weapons and personal treasure. And so that no one might know where he lay, the diggers were slaughtered and the waters of a river diverted over his grave to obscure the place forever.

The Visigoths never sailed to Africa. Athaulf, their new king, turned back through Italy. Desperate for food supplies and land his men could farm, Athaulf began to negotiate with the Emperor for estates they could peacefully settle. The Barbarian king took advice from Romans within his entourage, married a Roman princess, wore Roman dress and renounced his

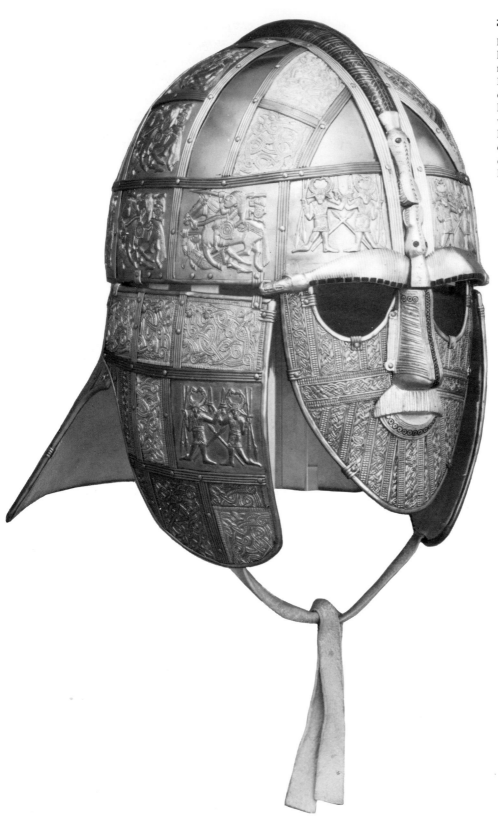

Replica of the warlord's helmet found at Sutton Hoo, made by the Tower of London Armourers. Panels decorating the side of the helmet show mounted warriors, lances in their hands, trampling down enemies. Elsewhere, dismounted warriors wear helmets with fantastic horns.

Helmet of iron, with gilt bronze face mask. Probably made in Sweden in the 6th century. Found at the ship burial of Sutton Hoo.

determination to smash *Romania* and set up *Gothia* in its place. In return for his support against other Barbarians, the Emperor granted the Visigoths a great chunk of southern France. Such a transition from foe to friend was not a smooth one. Athaulf could not control all his warriors. Those who still desired the life of a freebooter menaced southern France and had to be forcibly restrained. Assisted by their private armies, Romano-Germanic landowners spent much energy crushing the more anarchic members of their former Barbarian hordes. Throughout this period, the more remote corners of the land remained under the dominance of masterless bandits acting outside the interests of both the Emperor and German kings.

Alongside the mass accommodation of Barbarian tribes within the Empire, individual warriors offered their services to the Romans. Some acted as bounty-hunters, utilising their local knowledge to root out Barbarian marauders. Working outside the state, they were hired by groups of citizens or landowners to clear a certain district. Others were employed by the government, and information survives about one such man-hunter, Charietto. A German of fearsome reputation and appearance, he operated as a raider along the frontier near Trier with other Franks. Having exhausted the easy pickings, he rode into the provincial capital in the hope of hustling some money off citizens or troops in exchange for any form of service. Scouting, interpreting or perhaps, if he was lucky, even recruitment as an auxiliary with regular pay, food and a place to sleep. No official work offered itself, however, so he acted freelance. Realising very well that the surrounding countryside was plagued by Barbarian brigands – he had been among the most notorious of them – he set about making his experience pay. One night, he disappeared into the German forests and made for familiar bandit haunts. Around the dying embers of one camp-fire, he fell upon raiders drunkenly asleep after a successful day's work. He cut off their heads and, no doubt, snatched a few valuables for himself. Back in Trier he displayed the Barbarian heads and stirred the interest of the citizens. With a payment for each head delivered, Charietto embarked on a systematic annihilation of local outlaws. Soon his reputation persuaded others to stay away. At the same time, former bandits joined his gang of manhunters. Julian, commander of Roman forces along the Rhine, heard of Charietto's success and invited him to discuss tactics. The Franks, easily enough defeated in open confrontation, were resorting most sensibly to guerilla raids and proving elusive. Julian decided to harass the tribesmen during the day and then allow Charietto to stalk them at night. This combined pressure proved triumphant and Charietto rose to dizzy heights within the Imperial army. After a good ten years, however, his luck ran out in a bitter encounter with the Alamanni. Trying to encourage his fleeing men by confronting the enemy alone, he perished under several spears. Charietto was not an isolated example. Official bounty-hunting existed under the Emperor Valens who, during his war against the Goths, also offered a reward to anyone who brought in the heads of Barbarians.

Southern France was a vital part of the Western Empire. In the interior lay rich farmlands managed by some of the most powerful and wealthy Roman landlords. On the coast, the ports were an invaluable link in the chain of Mediterranean trade, the life-blood of the Empire. Weakened by civil wars that tore its armies apart and by Barbarian incursions that sprung up everywhere, the Imperial governors of Gaul abandoned a frontier policy. They could now no longer afford, or even admit it possible, to draw a line between the Barbaricum and the Empire. Instead, they rationalised the situation and saw that an Empire could still thrive – or rather, that its ruling class could endure – by adopting a new approach, an alternative definition of survival. The Empire invited Barbarians onto its territory. In this way, German chieftains then shared a common interest with Roman magnates in defending their way of life against the wreckers – savages with no respect for property or civilisation: although these 'savages' were merely those Barbarians who missed out on Roman patronage and were determined to

58

Pattern-welded sword in scabbard. Late 6th or early 7th century, from Sutton Hoo, Suffolk. Now in the British Museum, London.

gain a little treasure for themselves, with or without Imperial permission.

In the first half of the 5th century, the Visigoths were settled in Aquitaine around Toulouse. The Burgundians were invited into Savoy, south-eastern France, while groups of Alans were established in central France around Orleans. The Barbarians had not conquered these areas. They had been set up on Roman land in order to maintain a semblance of order and security, so that southern Gaul would remain an economically useful part of the Empire. For much of the time the Romanised Barbarians were not required to defend estates against invaders, but were used to crush the frequent revolts of heavily oppressed peasants and native Celts. To the outsider, it may have seemed as if France had fallen to the Barbarians but for Roman magnates and their German associates, it was, on the whole, business as usual. Only die-hard Imperialist historians, with their minds on an Augustan ideal of the 1st century, could really call this their blackest period. After all, the time spans discussed here were decades and warring was not constant. There were long stretches between major conflicts during which both Barbarian and Roman could concentrate on farming and trade. Then, the only fighting would have been riots and feuds sparked off by drunken disagreements between neighbouring landlords and their retinues. Even major confrontations, in truth, only involved warbands of a few hundred strong. The tribe in arms, a whole people taking the offensive, was a phenomenon of the past: and even then had been rare.

For German landholders and their supporters, war had become a professional occupation. They no longer fought to defend their families against Roman invaders. They no longer put down their plough to take up any weapon close to hand. From simple raiders they had emerged as a separate class, a ruling order of nobles and retainers. They no longer fought for cattle or slaves to sell to the Romans – their Gallic underlings dirtied their hands with soil and manure – they fought for the security of their property and landed income. Their weaponry reflected this privilege and pride. Leading German warriors wore shirts of mail. Long worn in the Roman army, mail was still a valuable item, and Frankish laws were later to proclaim a coat of mail worth two horses or six oxen. The making of mail took time and required special skills and tools. Roman mail workshops were well established, but it is not known to what extent this specialisation occurred amongst the Barbarians.

The construction of mail during this period probably differed little from later medieval examples. Essentially a defence of interlinked metal rings, one method of assembling mail used rows of solid rings linked with rings made from wire and closed with rivets. These latter rings were made by drawing metal wire through the progressively smaller holes of either a swage or a draw-plate. The wire was drawn through by hand or with a windlass. It was then coiled round an iron rod and cut up to form rings. Before being flattened for riveting, the ends of the rings were overlapped by being punched through a tapering hole in a steel block. The rings were

worked cold in all the processes so far described. As soon as the metal
became hard through working, it had to be heated red hot and left to cool.
The next stage, the flattening of the rivet joint, was achieved by placing the
ring between two steel dies and striking the top die with a hammer, thus
forcing the joint of the ring to take shape. Holes to take the rivets were
punched through the joints of the ring. Finally, the rings were opened and
linked together into the required formation. The rivets were then inserted
and closed. Each ring was linked with four others and was dense enough to
prevent the penetration of arrows or the slash of a sword. Surviving
examples of Roman mail are riveted and it is likely that much Barbarian mail
was as well. Oriental mail, however, had rings which are not overlapped
and riveted, but simply butted and some eastern Barbarian tribes may have
used this kind.

Early mail-makers used a soft iron ore. In order to toughen it, as was done
with swords and spear-heads, it was case-hardened. This was done by
rolling up the finished mail shirt in crushed charcoal and then placing it in a
forge until red-hot. The carbon in the charcoal turned the outside of the
iron into steel, the layer getting deeper the longer it was left. Weapons and
armour were rarely made of steel throughout, as this was likely to crack. In
the High Middle Ages, mail was decorated with rows of brass rings and this
was probably so in earlier centuries. Some of these brass rings were stamped
with talismanic words, these being hung near the most vulnerable spots.
Other rings were stamped with Christian monograms or the maker's mark.
The construction of a mail-shirt was undertaken by several people.
Apprentices did the repetitive, boring processes, while the master craftsmen actually 'knitted' it together. It is little wonder that a product of such
labour and technological expertise was highly valued and passed on from
father to son. Helmets were also precious. They were generally *Spangen-
helme*, built around an iron headband from which sprung strips of metal to

form a rounded cone. To this were riveted four to six bronze or iron plates. Hinged cheek-pieces, a strip of metal to protect the nose and a neck-guard of mail, were frequently added. Such a helmet was very strong and it is not surprising that this is the most characteristic helmet to survive from the period. As it was worn by kings and chieftains, it was often decorated with crests in the shape of boars, ravens and wolves. Images of power and magic.

Equally prestigious were the pattern-welded swords that belonged only to leading warriors. These blades had peculiar serpentine marks running down them that fired the imagination of their owners, leading to the swords being called names such as *Fishback* and *Dragonsword*. These blades were the result of the process of pattern-welding. When good quality steel was in short supply, smiths made blades out of a combination of light case-hardened iron and darker soft iron. These alternating layers of metal were sandwiched together, twisted and welded into one piece. Cutting edges of steel were separately welded onto this core. Half the total weight was then removed through grinding and the cutting edge filed. Finally, the blades were treated with an acid, anything from sour beer to urine, and the characteristic wavy pattern on the blade highlighted by etching and polishing. Some blades were made with a groove. Traditionally, this was supposed to allow the victim's blood to be channelled down the blade. Actually, its main function was to give extra strength to the edges without gaining weight or losing flexibility. A recent reconstruction of a pattern-welded sword took one craftsman 75 hours to complete, – from blade to belt-fittings. In Roman sword factories, such processes were handled by a team of artisans. Many such famous sword and armour workshops were taken over by the Barbarians in Italy and elsewhere.

Unlike other Barbarians, the Vandals found it difficult to settle down within the Empire. At the beginning of the 5th century, they along with Alans and the Suebi tore through Gaul and burst into Spain. Here they were harassed by Goths allied with Romans and pushed further into the peninsula. Compared to the Goths little is known about the Vandals. It seems likely that they, with an amalgam of other eastern Germans, operated as hordes of horse-warriors. Their action in Spain was far from a complete conquest. Areas held by strong Hispanic-Roman landlords channelled them towards weaker targets. Some cities held out against them. Their citizens riding out to hunt down isolated packs of the invaders. Occasionally the Empire sponsored other Barbarians, namely the Visigoths, to regain control of vital districts of the Mediterranean coast. Fighting was sporadic. Here and there a gang of raiders would be confronted by Spanish farmers or Imperial Germans. The Vandals do not appear to have gained the confidence of the Empire sufficiently to be employed themselves, or to be given land to defend. They were probably quite content to range over the wide lands of the peninsula as plunderers. Only twenty years after their first appearance south of the Pyrenees, a restless young generation pushed on across the sea to Africa. Apparently, they had been invited by a rebellious Roman warlord who then changed his mind — too late.

What the north-European Vandals made of the strange, hot lands of Africa is unknown. Though at this stage they were probably joined by rootless, marauding Spaniards and Moors who were more familiar with the new territory. Certainly, the Vandals were treated to yet another Roman province untouched by previous Barbarians and full of food and booty. But Africa was also over-flowing with fervent Catholicism and the conflict there soon developed into a desperate religious war between the bishops of each city along the Mediterranean coast and the fiercely Arian Vandals. The renowned Saint Augustine, bishop of Hippo, died during that city's siege. With the fall of each port, food supplies were cut to the rest of the Empire. Finally, with the seizure of Carthage, the Vandals were provided with a vast fleet, ready built and manned. Years before, the Romans had issued an edict promising death to anyone who revealed the secrets of shipbuilding to the Barbarians. Now the Vandals were fully equipped for a life of piracy. They raided Sicily and the coasts of Italy. Realising that his ports would be next, the Eastern Emperor dispatched two great armies to Africa: and this at a time when Constantinople was threatened by the Huns. The crisis escalated with the failure of these two expeditions. The Vandals in Africa were proving far more dangerous than they had ever been in Spain.

The main reason for the success of the Vandals lay in their king. Lame since a riding accident, Gaiseric was a highly able and respected statesman as well as warlord. He ruled for fifty years and led his people to their greatest victory. In 455, the Vandals sacked Rome. The whole of the Mediterranean was at their mercy. Western and eastern Roman fleets were crippled and destroyed. All the skills of naval warfare were revealed to them by captured Roman and Moorish sailors: including the secret of Greek Fire. Consisting of crude oils, pitch, fats, resins, sulphur and other inflammable, noxious ingredients, the mixture was poured into earthen-

The Vandals sack Rome in AD 455. From Ward Lock's *Illustrated History of the World*, 1885. Although nearly always depicted as northmen, the majority of the Vandal force would probably have been composed of native Spaniards and north Africans.

ware pots and ignited. Flung from ship-board catapults, the pots exploded on contact spraying a sticky, clinging, fiery substance over wood, canvas and skin. It even burnt on water, only sand could extinguish the flames. With their loss of Africa, and thus command of the Mediterranean, Roman Emperors began to comprehend that the Barbarians they felt sure they could control were now in a position to dictate the fate of the Empire to them. Such a suspicion became stone-cold fact in 476.

While Attila's kingdom was at its zenith, two men worked for him whose sons would play out the final drama of the Western Empire. One was a Roman, Orestes, who served as Attila's secretary, dealing with written requests sent to his illiterate master. The other was a Hun, Edeco, a respected warrior and leader of the horde. With Attila's death in 453, the two men were displaced in the anarchic power struggle that followed. Edeco joined the vagabond gangs of Huns who battled savagely with the Germans over food and territory. His son, Odoacer, fought at his side. Orestes made straight for the Western Empire where he served successfully in a military capacity. So useful was he that the Emperor gave him supreme command of the army in 475. But such power is too tempting and Orestes rebelled, setting up his son, Romulus, as Emperor. The boy was nicknamed Augustulus, 'little Augustus', because he was so young for the office. In the meantime, Odoacer had entered the army of Orestes as a promising captain. Ten months after the boy Emperor had been placed upon the throne, German soldiers under Odoacer protested that they should be allowed to have land to farm in Italy like the Visigoths had received in France. Orestes refused. Orestes was murdered. Mercifully, his young son was allowed to retire to a castle in the bay of Naples. He had no supporters. Romulus Augustulus was the last Roman Emperor of the West.

At the time, this deposition was considered nothing special. Contemporary chroniclers were not struck by it, for there had been gaps in the Imperial succession before. It was only with the passing of decades that the importance of the date was realised. By the next century, it was recognised as the end of the Western Empire. With no Imperial candidate and no Italian force strong enough to challenge him, Odoacer was proclaimed leader by his warriors. The Germans then settled their desired estates and Roman landlords soon accepted them in return for the stability and protection they provided. The Emperor of the East was politely informed that there was no need to look for a successor to his western counterpart. Odoacer would prefer to maintain his loyalty to one Emperor only. Although still legally part of the Empire, in reality, Italy had become a German kingdom. Admittedly a highly Latinised Barbarian domain, with Pope and senators still exercising influence, but nevertheless the peninsula could no longer be regarded as the heart of the Roman Empire. This was now wholly preserved in Constantinople. From there, the Empire prepared to strike back.

Alan and Sarmatian attacked by Hun. Eurasian steppeland, late 4th century. The Huns destroyed the realms of both the Alans and the Sarmatians.

Goth horse-warrior and foot-soldier ensnare a Roman legionary. Battle of Adrianople, AD 378.

Hun nobleman and raider ambushed by Balkan farmers, middle of the 5th century. The Huns carried bone-tipped composite bows.

Germans of the Cherusci tribe attack a Roman baggage train. Teutoburgian Forest, AD 9.

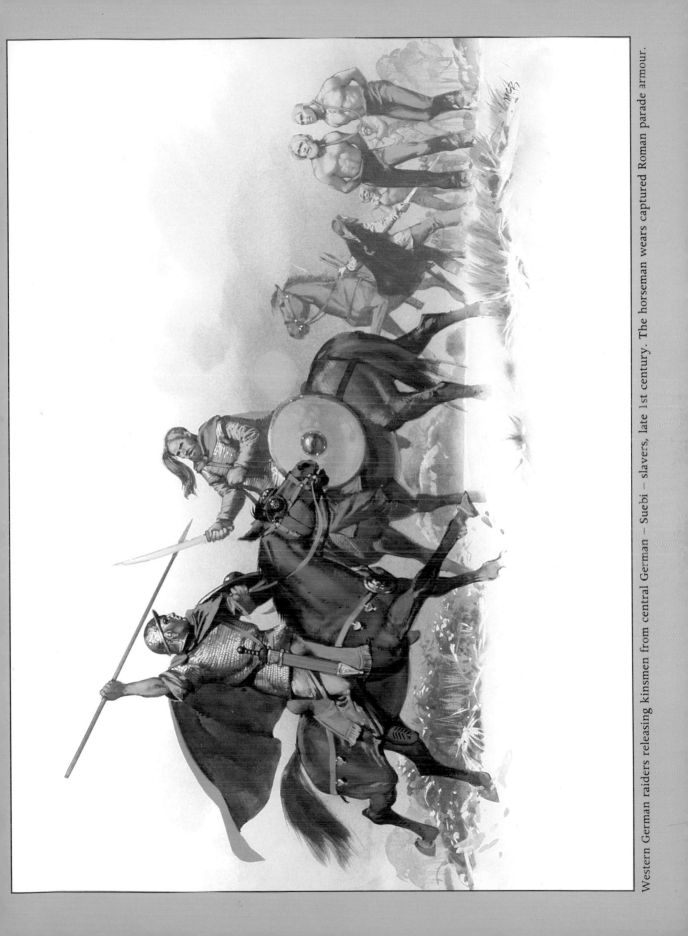

Western German raiders releasing kinsmen from central German – Suebi – slavers, late 1st century. The horseman wears captured Roman parade armour.

Visigoth bandits and runaway slaves ransack an Italian villa, early 5th century. The leading bandit has exaggerated his Barbarian image.

Gallo-Roman landlord hands over property rights to a Burgundian warlord. late 5th century.

Ostrogoths assault the Temple of Hadrian (now Castel S. Angelo), against a defence by citizens and Byzantine warriors. Siege of Rome, AD 537.

Franks attacking Byzantine warriors at the Battle of Casilinum, AD 554. Axe-wielding Frank foot-soldiers suffered heavily from enemy arrows.

Vandal raider shies away from Moorish warrior, Libyan desert, early 6th century. The Moors used camels within their tactical groups.

Muslim Arab warrior and his Ethiopian slave tackle a Sasanid Persian *clibanarium*. Mesopotamian desert, early 7th century.

Berber lancer and Arab archer clash with a Frank nobleman between Tours and Poitiers, AD 732. By this time some horsemen used stirrups.

Danish Viking chieftain and raider confronted by local Franks, Northern France, late 9th century. Viking raiders rode their stolen horses deep inland.

Swedish Vikings – Rus – board a Byzantine ship which is spraying Greek Fire through a dragon-shaped tube. The Black Sea, early 10th century.

Avar horse-warriors clash with the Carolingian Frank horsemen of Charlemagne, early 9th century, Bavaria.

German knights of the Teutonic Order confront heavily-armoured Mongol horse-warriors at the Battle of Liegnitz, 1241.

The Empire fights back

Behind the mosquito-infested marshes that surrounded and shielded Ravenna, Odoacer sat tight. Zeno, Emperor of the East, had broken the uneasy peace that lay between him and the West, and sent a Barbarian, Theoderic, to restore direct Imperial rule in Italy. Odoacer renounced all pretence of allegiance to Zeno and planned to make his own son Emperor of the West. By 489, Theoderic had Odoacer shut up in Ravenna. The siege dragged on for four years around the waters of the Po estuary until, in 493, a surrender was agreed. The two Barbarians were to rule as equals, but Theoderic could not forget the animosity and deaths that had separated them for so long. He invited Odoacer, now 60, to a feast. There, two men knelt before the veteran warlord and clasped his hands as they petitioned him for assistance. Thus shackled, warriors emerged from recesses in the walls of the Palace and prepared to strike the old man dead. They could not do it. Theoderic himself was forced to leap up and draw his sword. 'Where is God?' cried Odoacer. Tensing his muscles, Theoderic announced, 'I avenge my murdered friends so!' He brought his sword smashing down on Odoacer's collar-bone and cut deeply into his torso. Surprised at the depth of his blow, Theoderic bellowed, 'Indeed, this miserable man has no bones!'

For over thirty years, Theoderic ruled Italy as King of the Ostrogoths, the name given to the ragbag band of warriors that supported him. The Emperor of the East was no nearer to extending his control over the West than he had been under Odoacer. Theoderic reigned in all but name as Emperor of the West. As custodian of Italy for the Empire, he was careful to preserve Roman laws and estates, for while he was in command such administration was as beneficial to him as an efficient bureaucracy was to a medieval king. On the face of it, the Italians had little reason to overthrow their German master, particularly if it was only to exchange an approachable tyrant for one not even based on their own soil. Theoderic's pleas for tolerance, however, could not still the racial hatred that bubbled and often boiled over between Italian and German. Frequently, he had to compensate Roman land-owners for the unruly behaviour of his lower ranks. Gangs of

German warriors still roamed the peninsula in search of action and easy pickings, and were a constant irritation to the ruling order of Goths.

Unfurling a map of Europe, the new Emperor of the East, Justinian, and his Byzantine courtiers could see that more than half of the old Empire had been lost to the Barbarians. Britain was an assemblage of Saxon kingdoms: France was dominated by the Franks and Spain by the Visigoths: Africa was a firm base for the Vandals: while Italy was now under the sway of the Ostrogoths. Well, the Germans could keep Britain, it had always been a prestigious luxury, more trouble than it was worth. Similarly, the remoter tracts of France and central Europe were of little importance to the maintenance of Mediterranean trade. It was the coastal regions that had to be secured if the Empire was to enjoy continued economic supremacy. After having pacified the Persian frontier, Justinian sent his leading general to north Africa. In a lightning campaign, Belisarius, fast winning a reputation for exceptional military command, routed the Vandal kingdom and repossessed Africa. From there, all eyes focused on Italy. Could Justinian really rebuild the Roman Empire?

Like Germans before them, the Ostrogoths had a problem with Romanisation. Even before coming to Italy, Theoderic had enjoyed himself as a Roman patrician within the beguiling walls of Constantinople. So much so was he removed from the hardships of his people settled in the Balkans that he almost let slip his lordship of the Ostrogoths and had to drag himself away from the princely life of the Byzantines to lead his warriors westwards. Amongst his successors in Italy, that fatal attraction proved even more divisive. Theoderic's wife, Amalasuntha, roused the enmity of chief Goths by educating their son and hier as a civilised Roman. 'If fear of the schoolmaster's strap should overcome our young leader,' they argued, 'how could he possess the strength to defy the swords and spears of his enemies?' Amalasuntha, ruling as regent, despaired of the Barbaric interests of her inferiors and entered into secret negotiations with Justinian to return Italy to him. Likewise, other Goth magnates tried to sell Italy to the Byzantines for a guaranteed income and palace in Constantinople. All the fight had gone out of them. All they wanted was to retire in the lap of luxury and leave the suppression of peasants and marauders to the Emperor. Eventually, the murder of Amalasuntha before she could return Italy to him and the obvious dissension among the Goths, encouraged Justinian to embark on the reconquest of Italy.

Fresh from his success in Africa, Belisarius was appointed overall commander of the invasion force. In addition to his own private bodyguard – his retainers – his army of just over 7,000 men included regular Byzantine troops, Barbarian mercenaries, Isaurian mountain-men from Asia Minor armed with javelins, and small detachments of Moors and Avars. It was given out that his fleet was sailing to Carthage via Sicily. When Belisarius landed in Sicily, the reconquest had begun. In the meantime, to soften up the target, Justinian wrote to the Franks and offered them money if they would join in a general purging of the peninsula. The Franks hated the Goths and agreed. In Dalmatia, Imperial forces marched against Barbarians stationed there. In Sicily, all major cities yielded to Belisarius except one. A Goth garrison within Palermo refused to give up so easily. It was a strongly defended port and Belisarius decided to assault it from the sea. His ships sailed into the harbour and anchored right next to the city walls. The ships' sails overlooked the fortifications and the Byzantines exploited this ready advantage by hauling archers in little rowing boats way up to the top of the masts. From there the archers poured a hail of arrows into the Goths, and soon after the city opened its gates. By 536, Belisarius was lord of all Sicily.

Unfortunately for the Goths, at this time of crisis, their self-appointed leader was Theodatus. A wholly Romanised Barbarian, he was more interested in the philosophy of Plato than the defence of his people. Panicking, he wrote to Justinian with the plea, 'Let me hand over to you the whole of Italy, for I would rather live the life of a farmer free from all cares than persist in the dangers of remaining a king.' Justinian promised Theodatus a hefty annual pension and all the honours the Romans could bestow on him. For a moment, it seemed as if the reconquest of Italy would be an easier task than anticipated. However, as ambassadors took over from

The classic image of axe-wielding, fur-clad Barbarians, probably Franks. From Guizot's *L'Histoire de France*, 1870.

soldiers, news of a Goth counter-attack in Dalmatia emboldened Theodatus. It was now left to Belisarius to bring the Goths to heel.

On the mainland, the Byzantines were greeted by Italians from town and country. This may have been because few of the cities were fortified or garrisoned, and could not withstand Belisarius anyway. What Goths there were in the vicinity were surrendered immediately by their leader, in return for a boat to Constantinople. The Byzantines advanced along the west coast, accompanied by their fleet just offshore, until they reached Naples. The city was both fortified and garrisoned so Belisarius decided to enter into negotiations with the leading citizens to see if both sides could come to a mutually acceptable arrangement. One of the Neapolitans explained their situation frankly 'We are guarded by Barbarians and so cannot oppose them even if we wanted. These Goths, in turn, have left their families behind under the protection of Theodatus and so are not at liberty to betray him. It would be wiser for you to conquer Rome first, for then we would be encouraged to join you without a struggle. Otherwise, if you do not take Rome, you cannot expect to hold Naples'. Belisarius replied that he was determined on the capture of Naples and would rather treat the Neapolitans as friends than enemies – guaranteeing them safety from pillage. To the Goths, he offered either service with the Emperor or the freedom to go home to their farms. In addition, Belisarius promised the Neapolitan envoy great reward if he inspired good-will within the city.

The Neapolitans were divided. One side maintained that by remaining loyal to the Goths, they would not only be well treated if the Goth defenders were victorious but also in the event of defeat at least they would not be renowned as traitors, and so could be depended upon by the Emperor to accept the new regime without oppression. The Goth garrison promised these citizens a strong defence, while the Jewish community in the city made all their merchandise available. Belisarius was told to leave while the going was good. Enraged, the Byzantines flung themselves at the walls of Naples in an attempt to overcome it quickly. After this failed, they cut the aqueduct. The citizens survived from wells within the city.

As time rolled by, Belisarius despaired whether he would ever be rid of the Neapolitans, for he wished to engage Theodatus before the winter season. He prepared to leave the city. But then one of his warriors discovered a hole leading from the aqueduct into the city. This was made bigger and at night a contingent of Byzantines struggled through the tunnel. It was a covered aqueduct, supported by brick arches which carried it right into the middle of the city. Unable to emerge from it until they reached the end, the Byzantines then found themselves only able to get out of the tunnel by climbing on to an overhanging olive tree. This they did and advanced quietly through the streets to a tower in the wall. The defenders were slain and the Byzantines outside called to the wall. It was then discovered that their scaling ladders were too short. Carpenters had misjudged the height from afar, so they had to rope several together before the troops could ascend. The Byzantines on the wall patiently kept their cool and preserved their foothold. Fighting continued throughout the morning. The Neapolitan Jews, fearing an intolerant Christian regime, put up the stiffest resistance. Eventually, the city gates were thrown open and the whole Byzantine army burst in. The massacre, that Belisarius had hoped to avert, swept through the city as Imperial soldiers expended their frustration on the citizens. The Avars were said to be the most savage.

In Rome the Goths became openly dissatisfied with their leader when they heard that Naples had fallen. Theodatus seemed concerned only to remain as safe as possible, with as much money as possible. Sensing the increased animosity Theodatus fled – only to be tipped out of his carriage on the road to Ravenna where the fat man was murdered like an upturned turtle. A warrior, Vittigis, was then elected King of the Ostrogoths. Not a fool, he decided to finish off the conflict against the Franks before engaging in strength with Belisarius. He therefore gave up Rome to the advancing Byzantines and retreated to Ravenna. Vittigis had hoped that the Romans would remain loyal to him as he had treated them well, but on fearing that the fate of the Neapolitans would be inflicted on them if they held out, the citizens of Rome welcomed Belisarius through their gates. After sixty years, Rome was back under the direct control of the Empire.

Immediately, Belisarius set about restoring Rome's walls and fortifications. A deep moat was dug. Surrounding farmers were ordered to bring all their food to the great storehouses of the city. To this was added the grain the Byzantine fleet had brought from Sicily. Though impressed by the efficiency of these measures, the citizens were somewhat anxious at the

69

prospect of a siege. Their walls were too long to be defended at all points and provisions could not reach them from the sea. Compared with Naples, Rome was a sitting target. That said, the majority of Italians accepted the rule of Belisarius and were joined in this also by some Goths. Having strengthened their position up to and around the Tiber, the Byzantines now raided Tuscany and won several towns. Vittigis was being hemmed in. No longer content to sit it out in Ravenna, he sent a force to Dalmatia to recruit warriors from the Suevi, and to reclaim land lost by the Goths to the Empire. He bought a peace treaty with the Franks. Vittigis then gathered a massive army, claimed to be 150,000 strong, though this is obviously a wild exaggeration by Procopius, secretary and chronicler to Belisarius.

As Vittigis inspected his leading warriors, clad in mail which also covered their horses, he was furious that he had left it to this late stage to crush the invaders. He had heard that the Byzantine army was small and wished to march on Rome before Belisarius could retreat before his mighty horde. (Again, this may be Procopius underestimating his own forces so as to emphasise the generalship of his master.) It is likely that Belisarius' army was fairly large, as he would have been able to bolster his ranks with local men. Nevertheless, the Byzantine commander was apparently anxious at the speed of the Goth advance for he was expecting Imperial reinforcements. To slow down the Barbarians, he placed a garrison in a tower defending a bridge across the River Anio. The Goths camped before it, planning to storm it the next day. They were saved the trouble. That night, some of the terrified garrison, Barbarian by birth, deserted to the Goths, while others fled into the countryside. In the morning, unaware of his troop's desertion, Belisarius rode out with some horsemen to reinforce the bridge tower. Suddenly he was attacked by the Goths. Feeling his men waver, Belisarius charged into the midst of the action and engaged the enemy in combat. Deserters fighting with the Goths pointed out the general and soon all Barbarians were aiming their spears at the distinctive dark grey horse with white-flashed face. Belisarius' bodyguard desperately raised their shields around their master, for both sides knew that if he fell, the battle was over. Splattered in gore, Belisarius and his warriors turned this way and that as they hacked and thrust at the Goths. Eventually, the Byzantines fought their way back to the city. Many of Belisarius' closest and noblest warriors had fallen and though he had saved his troops from total annihilation, his actions were considered foolish by the Romans.

After this initial clash, the Goths settled in for a siege. They could not surround the entire length of the city walls and so throughout the spring of AD 537 they constructed six camps on the opposite side of the Tiber, where the Vatican now stands. The camps were fortified with trenches and mounds of earth in which were placed great numbers of wooden stakes. The Barbarians demolished some 14 ancient aqueducts that supplied the city with water and powered its mills. To obviate this, Belisarius set up the mill wheels on boats in the Tiber. The Goths simply broke these by throwing tree trunks and dead bodies into the river. This was countered by hanging great chains from a bridge that lay within the walls and thus collecting the rubbish.

Psychological warfare is particularly potent during a siege. The Goths realised this and exploited it fully. One night, a Goth chieftain rode up to the walls and denounced the Romans for their disloyalty to the Goths. 'Instead you have entrusted your father-land,' he shouted, 'to the Greeks. And the only Greeks you have seen before the arrival of Belisarius were thieving sailors and travelling actors!' Later, on hearing that the Romans were beginning to lose confidence in the Byzantines and resent Byzantine involvement of them in a siege, the Goths sent envoys into the city. 'Repent from your rashness,' urged the messengers, as if preaching to sinners. 'We have no argument with you. For have not the Goths in the past allowed you to live a life of freedom and luxury.' The citizenry were uncertain what to do. It was true that the oppression they now suffered under the military regime of the Byzantines was no better than the tyranny of the Goths which at least had allowed them to carry on their lives relatively free from rationing and assault. But they said nothing, no doubt afraid of the Byzantines, and the envoys returned to Vittigis saying that Belisarius was firm in his command of Rome.

The Goths prepared to storm the city. They revealed a competent knowledge of siegecraft and built great wooden, moveable towers, scaling ladders and battering rams. They filled in the moat with wood and reeds and on the eighteenth day of the siege began a general assault. On seeing the massive towers rumbling towards them, the Romans were dismayed. But Belisarius merely laughed. He ordered his archers to shoot at the oxen that pulled them forward. The great animals fell under the hail of arrows and prevented the towers from moving any nearer the walls. Those warriors who tried to remove the carcasses were also plied full of shafts. The towers stood there uselessly. Undeterred, at other points the Goths assembled in dense masses and rolled their battering rams against the walls. The Romans, in turn, activated their engines of war. One, called 'the wolf', consisted of iron-pointed beams which were suddenly allowed to fall on Barbarians nearest the wall. The beams plunged down and impaled many men on their metal beaks. On other occasions, they were used to smash the heads off battering rams.

Along some stretches of the wall, Vittigis commanded that his warriors restrain themselves from assault but just fire arrows at the battlements to prevent the Byzantines from moving along them and reinforcing other sections under attack. By so doing, the Barbarians made themselves vulnerable to the Romans' *ballistae* and catapults. Firing iron-tipped shafts with double the power of a normal bow, the *ballistae* proved lethal. One Goth, a noble warrior wearing a breastplate, separated himself from his comrades and stood against a tree trunk. From there he placed many arrows accurately amongst the defenders. Aggravated, some Byzantines directed

Silver-inlaid sword hilt of the 7th century. From southern Germany, now in the State Prehistorical Collection, Munich.

their *ballista* at this sharpshooter. A few moments later, a bolt flashed out and plunged through the Goth's armour with such force that it pinned him against the tree, leaving the dead man suspended. His fellow warriors moved out of range.

The Romans and the Byzantines considered themselves supreme at siege-warfare and accounts of Barbarian incompetence while assaulting towns frequently have the air of black comedy about them. Dexippus described a siege of Philippopolis in which the Goths spent much time painstakingly constructing wooden shelters covered with hides to protect them against the fiery missiles of the defenders. Their warriors got inside the boxes and were wheeled to the city gates. Here, the citizens simply heaved great stones up onto the battlements and dropped them on their attackers. Both boxes and Barbarians were crushed. But were the Barbarians always that stupid? On many occasions they do seem to have been overawed by superior Roman military technology and tended to restrict their initial campaigns to raiding easier targets: countryside villas and towns without walls. By the 5th century, however, the Barbarians did attack major cities and with success. Even the Huns, supposedly the most primitive and least equipped Barbarians made city gates shake.

When Attila invaded France, Orleans nearly fell to his battering rams. Later, major urban centres of northern Italy were devastated. Priscus, a highly reliable chronicler of events in his own day, records a successful Hun assault on the city of Naissus in 441. The Huns brought great engines of war against the circuit walls. Wooden planks mounted on wheels allowed Hun archers to be pushed forward under cover of screens made of interwoven willow twigs and rawhide. Other engines included massive metal-tipped battering rams swinging on chains. Men at the back of a ram, protected again by screens, pulled back ropes attached to the beam and then let it crash against the wall. Eventually parts of the city walls were broken down and Huns with scaling ladders brought the siege to a bloody conclusion. At this stage, one might suspect that the Barbarians were helped in technological matters by Roman prisoners and deserters. This may be true but it is also likely that the majority of Barbarians did have a good grasp of siegecraft and that the continued Roman denigration of Barbarian achievements was merely prejudiced elitism. Besides, there were many other ways a city could fall into the hands of the enemy. Surprise, panic, mismanagement, blockade and treachery all brought cities to their knees. In the 6th-century siege of Rome, however, the Ostrogoths were confident enough of their skills to hope for victory by direct assault.

While Roman war machines kept many Barbarians away from the walls, the Goths had more success elsewhere, around the Tomb of Hadrian. A massive marble monument surmounted by statues, the mausoleum had been incorporated as a tower into the city's defences. While their archers tried to clear the battlements, the Goths rushed forward. Some, partly hidden by a colonnade leading from the church of St Peter, held very long, man-size shields. These proved highly effective against the defenders' arrows and allowed them to raise their ladders against the walls. The Byzantines manning the Tomb were almost surrounded and out of desperation they began to break up the statues they had been pushed back amongst. Hurling lumps of marble down on the Goths, the attackers were battered, crushed and forced back. Where Goths tried to under-mine the walls, Byzantines fought hand to hand through the holes and threw them out. By the end of the day, the Goths were licking their wounds while the Romans were singing loudly the praises of Belisarius.

Though pleased with the action so far, Belisarius realised he needed more men and wrote urgently to Justinian. To bolster his forces, before the arrival of reinforcements, Belisarius enrolled all able-bodied Romans into his army. At the same time, to save their scanty food supplies, Belisarius ordered the evacuation of all women and children to Naples. This could be done because the Goth forces were not large enough to surround the whole city. Indeed, to protect themselves from Byzantine counter attacks they had restricted themselves to a few fortified camps on just one side of the city. In order to capitalise on this fear, the Byzantines sent out gangs of Moors with hunting dogs to pounce upon isolated groups of Barbarians. The Moors, renowned for their savagery, stripped their victims and then ran speedily back to the walls. Such a situation allowed Rome to receive regular provisions.

To prevent the city being given up by treachery, Belisarius banished all suspect Romans and changed the locks of the gates frequently. To Vittigis, it seemed as if the siege could go on forever. In his frustration, he slaughtered many hostages he had captured before the war. News of this only strengthened the citizens resolve. So Vittigis decided to cut some of the Byzantine supply routes and successfully captured the port of Rome some miles from the city. Belisarius had been unable to spare any troops to garrison it. At this dire moment, Byzantine reinforcements suddenly arrived. Not a major force – sixteen hundred Slav and Avar horsemen – but it was enough for Belisarius to consider carrying the battle outside the walls and against the Goths. In the following skirmishes, the essential differences between Western and Eastern warfare were clearly demonstrated.

A few hundred Byzantine horsemen dashed out of the city and rode towards the Goth camps. They were given strict instructions not to engage the Barbarians in close combat but to use their bows only. Provoked, the Goths grabbed any weapon to hand and rushed out to meet them. The Byzantines evaded their charges and rode onto a hill from where they shot arrows at the advancing crowd of Goths. As soon as their quivers were exhausted, they galloped back to the city walls, chased hotly by wounded and furious Barbarians. From their battlements, the Romans covered their horsemen with *ballistae* bolts. Yet more Goths fell under the vicious storm. Twice more Belisarius executed this tactic with great loss to Vittigis. If Procopius is to be believed, and he is most certainly an eye-witness to the

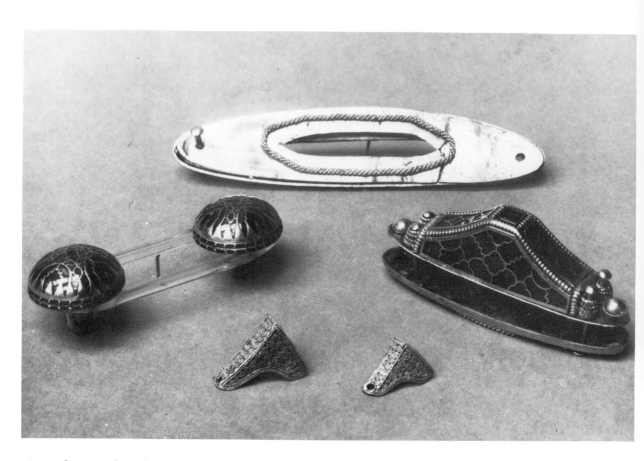

siege of Rome, then the point of these confrontations was that the Goths did not possess horse-archers with which to counter the Byzantines. Like all western German tribes – the Franks and Saxons included – Goth horse-warriors wielded sword and spear only, while the majority of their armed forces fought on foot with spears. Though they had lived for many years in eastern Europe, in close contact with the horse-archers of the Huns and Sarmatians, the Goths do not seem to have adopted the bow as a weapon worthy of the mounted warrior. Bows were used by Goth foot-soldiers and appear throughout the siege of Rome, though these were most probably simple wooden bows, like those found in northern Europe, and not composite bows. The fact remains, however, that Goth horse-warriors resolutely refused to combine the power and range of the bow with the mobility of their mount.

Gold sword fittings inlaid with garnets from the Sutton Hoo ship burial. Late 6th or early 7th century, possibly Swedish.

The reason for this prejudice among German horse-warriors against using bow and arrow appears to be a purely cultural affectation. It seems to have been deeply inbred among the aristocratic ranks of Germanic Barbarians that it was not manly to fire at the enemy from afar. Martial glory could only be obtained through the slogging exchange of sword against spear. This western aversion to the mounted archer defied all military logic and experience. Again and again, when keeping at a distance, horse-archers from the East – whether Hun, Byzantine or Avar – soundly thrashed their Germanic counterparts.

Such a social prejudice against the bow determined the whole nature of western warfare for the next thousand years. Throughout the Middle Ages, it was considered unseemly for a knight to use a bow and arrow, and in later centuries this applied to firearms. Even when the Crusader knights fought in the Holy Land against highly effective Turkish horse-archers, they clung faithfully to their swords and lances. It was left to their foot-soldier underlings to return fire with bow and crossbow. It is a peculiarity of medieval western European warfare that the high social standing of the horse-warrior – the knight – meant that he could not contemplate using the weapons of his inferiors. Elsewhere in the world, where the riding of a horse was somewhat less of a mark of social rank, the bow was an essential arm of even the most noble warrior: the most excellent and decorated bows being highly prized. In the west, there were no decorated or gilded bows. The only occasion when a western aristocrat might bring himself to touch a bow was in hunting or sport. But never in battle. As a result, exceptions to this rule stand out. In his 6th century Frank chronicle, Gregory of Tours mentions that Count Leudast wore a quiver hanging round his mail shirt. In all other respects, the Count was patently a member of the elite warrior class – his breastplate, his helmet, his mail – and yet he also carried a bow. Perhaps this detail was intended to show that he was a parvenu: he had risen quickly from cook to stablemaster to count and so did not possess the decorum of truly noble men. Perhaps the social and military situation during this period was sufficiently fluid to allow for such a transgression: military snobbery became more rigid throughout the Middle Ages. Whatever the explanation, this was most unusual and the noble horse-warrior, with sword and lance only, dominated western, Germanic warfare for centuries to come. With such a fundamental handicap, it is remarkable that the Goths ever won any conflict with eastern warriors. But they did, maintaining the war against the Byzantines for many years. The answer to this lies in the fact that few military combats are planned, text-book battles. Surprise and a rapid rush into hand-to-hand fighting quashed any advantage horse-archers might have possessed over Germanic horsemen.

Elated by the success of their skirmishes against the Goths, the Romans wished to finish the siege of their city with a pitched battle outside the walls. Belisarius was reluctant to risk his whole army in such an engagement, but eventually acceded to the enthusiasm of the citizens. For several days, the battle was delayed because Byzantine deserters kept informing the Barbarians of the offensive. When the confrontation at last began, a lack of professionalism and control proved crucial to the outcome. Belisarius wished to fight a cavalry battle and many of his foot-soldiers rode on captured horses. Their archery proved effective and slew great numbers of the massed Barbarians. Elsewhere on the battlefield, crowds of Roman citizens, demanding to carry arms and fight alongside the regular Byzantine troops, became excited at the apparent defeat of the Goths and rushed upon them. Surprised, the Goths fell back. The charging mob of Roman citizens, servants, sailors and artisans pursued them as far as their camps, but allowed the Goths to retreat into the hills while they looted their wagons and tents. Seeing the collapse of the Roman advance into a chaos of pillage, the Barbarians, full of fury and shouting terribly, dashed down the hill-sides and savaged the plunderers. At the same time, the initial onslaught of the Byzantines had come to a halt and now Goth horse-warriors galloped to assault them with spears and lances. The lighter spears were thrown, while the heavier lances were held in two hands and carried into close combat. A general retreat soon escalated into a rout as horrified Romans threw the Byzantines into disorder in their sprint to the safety of the city walls. After this disaster, Belisarius resumed his smaller, sudden sallies of horse-archers.

The siege of Rome dragged on for a year until the spring of 538. Long periods of famine and disease were broken occasionally by reports of the bold exploits of members of Belisarius' bodyguard. This elite corps frequently amazed the Romans and Byzantines with their daring acts of solitary courage. On one occasion, Chorsamantis, an Avar, wounded and drunk, rode out by himself to the Goth camp. At first, the Barbarians thought he was a deserter, but then he raised his bow. Arrows flashed towards them. Twenty Goths immediately galloped out. Chorsamantis swung his spear at these men with such ferocity that while some fell dead, others shied away. Cursing the weakness of the Germans, he turned round and trotted back to the city. Insulted, other Goths charged after him. Watching from their battlements, Byzantines shouted words of encouragement as the Avar wildly deflected the blows of the Barbarians. Swords and spears clattered against mail. The Avar seemed raving mad in his superhuman energy. Eventually he was surrounded and crumpled beneath the cuts of his team-handed adversaries. At another time, it was a Thracian who deeply impressed his fellow warriors. In order to keep the Barbarians occupied during an Imperial delivery of money for the troops, a group of Byzantine horsemen rode out to the Goth camp. In the skirmish that followed, Cutilas, another of Belisarius' bodyguard, was struck in the forehead by an arrow. Undeterred, he forced back his assailants and chased after them. Returning to the city, the whole arrow remained in the Thracian's head, waving about to the astonishment of the Romans. Clearly, the Germans were not the only people to appreciate or originate tales of heroic single-combat.

Barricaded in their fortified camps against the relentless raids of the Byzantines, the Goths felt as besieged as the Romans. Having already plundered all local farmland, the Barbarians were also suffering from famine and plague. The arrival of Byzantine reinforcements further demoralised the Goths and an armistice was called between the two forces in order to work out a compromise. The Byzantines took advantage of this pause and improved their position throughout central Italy, taking over towns evacuated by the Goths. Vittigis, the Goth leader, tried a few more feeble attempts to breach the walls of Rome but eventually the Goths gave up and retreated to Ravenna. The siege of Rome ended with no titanic battle, but merely fizzled out through exhaustion. Over the next years, scattered, chaotic fighting embroiled the whole of northern Italy. Milan, the second largest city in Italy, was lost to an allied force of Goths and Burgundians. All male citizens were massacred and the women given as slaves to the Burgundians: just one of many atrocities in a savage war. Amidst this brutality, Belisarius maintained his upper hand, and finally captured Ravenna. Vittigis was sent to Constantinople.

Fearful that Belisarius had grown too powerful through his victories, and might assume control as Emperor of the West, the Emperor Justinian recalled him. Soon after Belisarius left Italy, however, the few remaining Goth strongholds broke out and defeated piecemeal the Imperial garrisons scattered throughout the land. And then in 545, the new leader of the Goths, Totila, captured Rome. All the effort and sacrifice that had gone into the reconquest of Italy had been lost in only a few years. All because of the Emperor's jealousy and suspicion.

Belisarius was sent back to Italy, but because Justinian still did not trust him, he was provided with a wholly inadequate army. Rome was re-captured, but the war degenerated into a savage game of hide and seek with the population of Italy suffering terribly at the hands of rampaging Byzantines and Goths. Again Belisarius was recalled to Constantinople and once again the Goths emerged to seize territory lost to the Imperialists. Though a statesman of great vision and enterprise, Justinian let his personal jealousies lose him any gains. Finally, however, he realised that Italy could only be secured by a major and decisive campaign. The eunuch warlord Narses was put in command of a substantial army of around 25,000. On his way to Rome in 552, he confronted a smaller force of Barbarians near the village of Taginae. Situated high in the Apennines, the Byzantines positioned themselves amongst the mountain crevasses and awaited the Goths. A tactically-vital prominence was guarded by fifty Byzantine foot-soldiers. The next day, the Barbarians also realised the importance of this hill and before the main combat broke out, Totila sent forward a group of horsemen to capture it. They dashed up the mountain slope, brandishing their spears and yelping fiercely. The Byzantines, however, were drawn up in a tight phalanx. The Goth horses stopped abruptly and swerved away from the formidable wall of shields and spears. Several times the Goth horse-warriors tried to break the resolve of the foot-soldiers, but each time they were repulsed. Among the Byzantines, one soldier particularly distinguished himself. With his quiver empty and his sword bent, he grabbed the Goth spears with his bare hands and wrenched them from the Barbarians. In recognition of this bravery, Narses appointed the warrior to his personal bodyguard. Thus a warlord insured his own protection by being surrounded by only the most courageous warriors.

Both sides prepared for battle. Narses and his personal retainers, as well as his finest regular soldiers, positioned themselves around the hill. On each flank, Narses placed contingents of dismounted Byzantine archers. Bracing themselves on foot, these men could use stronger bows than horsemen and so had a greater range. A group of cavalry were maintained in reserve to reinforce the main body and execute encircling manouevres when the enemy were engaged. In the centre, between him and his right wing, Narses assembled his German mercenaries, among them both Lombards and Heruli. He dismounted this essentially horse-borne force because he felt they were untrustworthy and less likely to flee if on foot. The Lombards were such a wild tribe, ravaging and assaulting the native Italians wherever they went, that after the battle Narses was forced to send them back to their own land. Totila similarly organised his army with a phalanx of foot-soldiers flanked by bands of horse-warriors. As each side readied itself for combat, praying and chanting, a Goth rode out from his ranks and challenged the Byzantines to a duel. The Goth happened to be a Byzantine deserter and immediately one of Narses' bodyguard rode forward. The Goth charged, trying to ram his spear into the Byzantine's stomach. The Byzantine turned his horse aside and the Goth lurched past harmlessly. The Byzantine then thrust his own spear at the Barbarian's side and the Goth fell to the ground. A tremendous shout arose from the Byzantine army. They were ready to fight.

With such a dire omen, Totila wished to delay the battle and buy time as he knew reinforcements were close at hand. Desperately, Totila dashed out into the space between the two forces. Clad in gold-plated armour and with regal purple ornaments hanging from the cheek-pieces on his helmet, the Goth warlord hurled his spear into the air and caught it skilfully. At the same time, he wheeled his horse around in a kind of dance. Continuing to juggle his spear, he then leaned back on his horse and stretched out his legs, just as if a trick rider in a circus act. Amazed and somewhat bemused by this performance, the Byzantines held back. With the addition of two thousand Goths who arrived during his performance, Totila armed himself for battle. He pulled on a simple mail shirt and dressed himself as an ordinary warrior so he would not be a conspicuous target for the enemy. The armies then moved towards each other.

According to their orders, Narses' flanking archers advanced further than the rest of the Byzantines. Into this crescent galloped the Goth nobles and their horse-warriors, the foot-soldiers following behind. Rashly, and no doubt because of his Germanic pride, Totila commanded that his warriors should not use bows or any other weapon except their spears. It is difficult to believe that warriors fighting for their life would obey such a silly conceit. Perhaps this was an attempt by Procopius, the chronicler of the battle, to explain the absence of the bow amongst Goth horse-warriors. Whatever happened, the Goths were suddenly raked by a murderous rain of arrows from Byzantines on each side. Losing many warriors, the Goths clashed ineffectively with Narses' dismounted German spearmen, while

Belisarius leads his warriors against the Ostrogoths. From Ward Lock's *Illustrated History of the World*, 1885.

78

the Byzantine cavalry endeavoured to encircle them. As the afternoon drew to an end, those Goth horsemen that remained rushed back onto their foot-soldiers, who broke before the general advance of the Byzantines. Throughout the night, gangs of Byzantines and Germans chased fugitive Goths, amongst them Totila. Caught up with, the Goth king and his retainers were slain.

After such a victory, Narses marched on Rome. For the fifth time in Justinian's reign, the city was recaptured. From there, Narses fought a last battle with the Goths around their treasure store in the stronghold of Cumae. In the shadow of Mt Vesuvius, the two forces dismounted because of the rough terrain. The battle centred around the figure of the newly elected Goth king, Teias. After losing many men in the process, the Byzantines finally obtained the head of Teias and displayed it on a pole to

the Goths, hoping that they would then surrender. The Barbarians, however, were intent on a desperate last-stand and the fighting continued until the next day. Eventually their position was recognised as hopeless and a number of Goth chieftains swore on their swords to stop fighting in exchange for safe conduct out of the peninsula. The majority of Goths were escorted out of Italy and the reign of the Ostrogoths was broken. Italy was now ruled directly from Constantinople and was again part of the Roman Empire. This had taken twenty years to achieve and the farmers and citizens of Italy had been wracked by military savagery, famine and disease. There was nothing to celebrate. And still the war for Italy was far from over. No sooner had Narses crushed the remaining Goth outposts, than the Franks decided to embark on a major invasion of the peninsula.

The Franks were a confederation of Barbarians composed of ferocious western German tribes that Tacitus had referred to in the 1st century. 'These Franks were called *Germani* in ancient times,' Procopius announced. Like all western Germans, a majority of Franks fought on foot, while their leading horse-warriors carried spears and swords but no bows. In addition to this basic armament, the Franks were renowned for their battle-axes. The *francisca* was an iron-headed, short-handled, throwing axe. According to Procopius and Agathias, it was double-edged, although archaeological finds show that some possessed a single blade. In battle, the Franks hurled these axes at the enemy as they charged forward. The Franks were noted also for their use of a javelin, called an *ango*. This had a barbed iron head that ran someway down its shaft so that its head could not be chopped off. It was modelled on the Roman *pilum* and Agathias, writing in the 6th century, suggested that it could be used in a similar way. When the javelin struck an enemy shield, it was not easily removed and weighed down the shield, thus allowing Frankish warriors to strike the unprotected foe.

Throughout the 5th century, the Franks had made great inroads into Gaul and established it as their country. They defeated the Gallo-Roman landowners, and in 507, at the battle of Vouillé, they shattered the Visigoths settled in the south of France. The Goths retreated into Spain, where they remained during the 6th and 7th centuries. Around the beginning of the 6th century, in their wars against the Alamanni, the Burgundians and the Visigoths, the Franks were led by the energetic and ruthless Clovis. He was the grandson of Meroveus, a chieftain who had fought alongside Aetius against Attila in 451 and given his name to the Merovingian dynasty. It was Clovis who welded the Franks into a unified force and established the Merovingians as its ruling family. He killed those Franks who opposed him and absorbed their land and wealth. He commanded through terror. On one occasion he addressed his warriors on the fact that he, as chieftain, should receive more booty than the rest. One warrior disagreed and stated that they should all receive an equal share. Clovis hid his anger and passed on to other matters. Some months later, when he was inspecting his warriors' arms, he came across the warrior who had denied him his extra share.

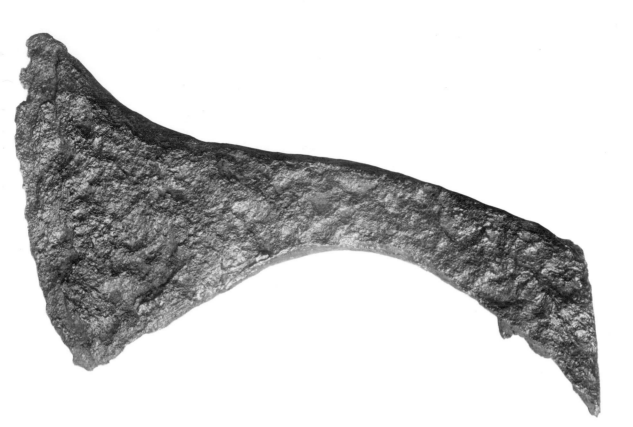

The single-edged blade of the *francisca* throwing axe, characteristic of the Franks. Found at Howletts, Kent, now in the British Museum, London.

Criticising the condition of the warrior's spear, sword and axe, Clovis threw the latter weapon on the ground. The warrior bent to pick it up and as he did so, Clovis raised his own battle axe and split open the warrior's skull. The rest of his men took heed of this warning. With his conversion to Catholicism, and his acceptance of a consulship from the Eastern Emperor, Clovis and his clan became the official rulers of France. Clovis' attitude to religion encouraged cynicism. Of the Visigoths he said, 'I cannot bear to see those Arians occupying any part of Gaul. With God's help, we will invade them and when we have beaten them, we will take over their territory.'

The official recognition of Clovis by the Eastern Emperor was most likely a Byzantine ploy to counter the power of the Goths in the west. Throughout the reconquest, the Franks loomed over north-west Italy, changing their allegiance as it suited their ambitions. Occasionally, they carried out raids against the Byzantines as well as the Goths. With the death of Clovis in 511, his kingdom was divided equally, according to Frank law, among his four sons. Such an inheritance weakened the unity of the Franks and there was much feuding. Nevertheless, their energy was also directed against outsiders and the kingdoms of the Franks remained a strong European power. In 553, Frank warlords invaded Italy and were joined by remnants of the vanquished Ostrogoths. They rode through Italy and ravaged many

Byzantine garrisons. Narses bided his time and built up his strength. The next year, Narses confronted the Franks at the Battle of Casilinum. Horse-archers annihilated the invading troops. Remaining Frank bands were decimated by epidemic and Italy was again left to the Byzantines. For just over ten years, Italy remained free of Barbarians. Justinian, and his courtiers in Constantinople, probably marvelled at the fact that he had done more than any other late Roman Emperor to rebuild the glory of Rome. And yet Italy was too vulnerable to be long out of German hands. Shortly after Justinian's death in 565, his Empire began to crumble. Retreating before the Avars, the Lombards crossed the Alps in 568 and set in motion a series of wars with the Byzantines that lasted for two centuries and forced the Imperialists into southern Italy. Ravenna remained an isolated outpost of the Empire in the north, while the Popes in Rome stiffly resisted the Arian Lombards.

As with other German invasions, the Lombard incursion was largely a contest for the most attractive landholdings. Lombard nobles competed with Byzantine landowners, and in their wake left the ruined lives of more humble Italians. On every occasion, it was the peasants who suffered most from marauding gangs of Barbarians and Imperialists. By this time, despairing of ever aligning themselves with the right side, they maintained an open hostility to both oppressors. Italy was a land fought over, not governed. Wars of conquest merely gave way to ferocious vendettas between landlords. In between fighting, Lombard aristocrats continued the business of their predecessors: exporting and importing goods from Italian ports and maintaining trade from farm to town. In many respects, aside from the ever-present power struggle over who claimed what piece of land, the Germans, the Byzantines and the descendants of the old Imperial ruling caste settled down to a way of life that was very similar to – and a continuation of – the Roman economy. In the 7th century, however, their monopoly of the Mediterranean was severly disturbed by a new power from the East. A froce motivated by the word of God.

The force of God

THE
MOORS
AND ARABS:
THE
7th AND 8th
CENTURIES

In a cave in the mountains of western Arabia, a man received messages from God. Within twenty years of announcing these visions, Arabia had been converted to a new religion and united under this one man. Within fifty years, his successors conquered Palestine, Syria, Mesopotamia, Egypt, Persia and Afghanistan. The Persian Sasanid Empire was annihilated and the Byzantine Empire left with only one oriental province in Asia Minor. Within a hundred years of that lonely mystical experience, the followers of the Messenger of God ruled a domain that stretched from India to Spain and from the Sahara to southern France and Central Asia. In a remarkably brief period, Arabs held sway over lands on three continents: an area vaster than that controlled by the Romans at the height of their Empire. The Messenger of God was Muhammad and his religion — Islam.

For centuries before their surrender to Islam, the nomadic tribes of Arabia were considered of little importance. To the Roman and Persian empires the wild Arabs of the interior were vagabonds whose raids were ineffectual pin-pricks: nothing to worry about. Occasionally the tribes fought for Imperial forces but always they disappeared back into the desert. In the 6th century, it was the Moors, the native inhabitants of Mauretania — the western regions of north Africa — who proved the most dangerous of the southern Barbarians, but even they were dismissed by the Byzantines as the most poorly armed Barbarians the Empire had to fight. Solomon, commander of Byzantine forces in north Africa after Belisarius, described the Moors thus, 'Most of them have no armour at all. Those that have shields, have only small, poorly made ones which are not able to turn aside thrusts against them. They carry only two short spears and once they throw these, if they achieve nothing, they turn around and run.'

Solomon underrated the Moors at his own cost. Later they ambushed him and he was killed. Indeed, in the competition for power following the death of Gaiseric, the great Vandal leader, the Moors inflicted several serious defeats on the Germanic Barbarians. One of the most devastating was won by Cabaon in Libya.

For days, Cabaon had been aware that the Vandals were advancing into his territory. He had sent spies into Carthage and was well informed of the Vandal raids. In order to obtain supernatural support and also, no doubt, to gain the friendship of local inhabitants, he instructed his spies to help those Roman Christians assaulted by the Arian Germans. After each violent attack on a church or Catholic community, Cabaon's agents moved in, cleared up the damage and recompensed the holy men for their losses. In the meantime, the Moor leader ordered his warriors to abstain from all injustice, all luxurious foods and, most of all, association with women. To reinforce this order a palisade was set up between the men and women in his camp. Women and children remained with their men on campaign so they could tend horses and camels, construct stockades and sharpen weapons. When Cabaon's spies finally told him that the Vandals were fast approaching, he prepared his warriors in the usual Moorish fashion. Their camels were rounded up in a circle, twelve animals deep. Warriors, wielding swords and javelins, stood amongst them. Confronted with the sight and smell of these camels, the horses of the Vandal raiders shied away and refused to be driven towards them. Some horses panicked and threw their perplexed riders to the ground. Without bows or effective missile weapons, the Germans suffered badly from the showers of javelins hurled at their ranks. Unable to return the fire, the resolve of the Vandals disintegrated and they broke before the advancing Moors.

With the conquest of the Vandals by Belisarius, the Moors tried out the same tactics against the Byzantines. Against a more sophisticated force, they came unstuck. Quickly appreciating the effect of camels on their horses, the Byzantine cavalry dismounted and marched towards the Moors with their shields interlocked in a powerful wall of wood and iron. The light Moorish spears bounced off the heavily armoured warriors and when they reached the lines of camels, the warriors slaughtered both the animals and the men hiding behind them. The Moors fled and the Byzantine horsemen, now regaining their mounts, cut down many in the pursuit. From then on the Moors avoided pitched battles in open spaces and concentrated on damaging raids. Though unable to throw the Byzantines out of north Africa, the Moors nevertheless remained a constant problem to the Empire. When the Empire withdrew before the Arabs, the Moors joined the great surge of Islam and went on the offensive against Europe.

The Roman and Persian empires had never bothered to conquer the whole of the Arabian peninsula. In the interior, deserts and arid mountains encouraged a nomadic pastoral existence. Arabia's only source of wealth and appeal to outsiders was its many trade routes which crossed the land from the south and the Indian Ocean. Caravans laden with aromatic and exotic goods advanced from oasis to oasis along the Red Sea coast. Around these fertile pools thrived market towns that grew fat on the trade that passed through them. Frequently, neighbouring towns competed violently with each other to ensure that caravans paused with them rather than their rivals. In a battle to secure their monopoly over the middle stretch of the Incense Route, the merchants of Mecca defeated the people of Tā'if, a few miles to their east. By the beginning of the 7th century Mecca was a major commercial centre, deriving its great wealth almost exclusively from the caravan trade. To ensure its continued prosperity, Bedouin nomads from the interior were employed as guards and guides for the myriad trains of camels that passed to and fro. Occasionally, and more as a sport and demonstration of masculine prowess, Arab townsmen would engage in raids – called *razzias* – on neighbouring communities. The intention was to avoid bloody confrontation and simply rustle a few animals from their rivals.

It was into this world of high materialism that Muhammad, a man of middling status and wealth, was born. By 610, in his late middle-age, he began to preach to the citizens of Mecca about his mystical experiences. These revelations became the essential tenets of the Koran and Islam, an offshoot of the Jewish and Christian religions. Muhammad preached that God – Allah – is almighty and that he alone should be worshipped. After a

Parthian horse-archer. The Parthians had been the great eastern enemies of Rome until displaced by the Persian Sasanid dynasty. Terracotta image, 1st to 3rd century AD, now in the British Museum, London.

period of toleration, the Jews were accused of corrupting the scriptures, while the Christians were criticised for worshipping Jesus as the Son of God. Muhammad was only a prophet – a messenger – he was not of supernatural origin. In addition to this basic faith in one God, Muhammad taught that God expected his people to be generous with their wealth; to help those less fortunate than themselves. In return those people that led a virtuous life would, on the Day of Judgement, pass in to heaven, while those who had not, would be consigned to hell. Such a blatantly anti-materialist philosophy naturally excited the poor of Mecca and annoyed the ruling merchants. Irritation turned to outright hostility and in 622, Muhammad and his Muslim followers fled to Medina, the next important trade centre, 200 miles to the north of Mecca. It is from this date that Islamic history begins – year one.

Instead of settling down to a life of meditation and preaching in Medina, Muhammad at once began organising raids against Meccan caravans. Ostensibly to gain his impoverished followers a living in a new town, it seems likely that Muhammad also used these raids as a method of building up his power and respect in Medina, and amongst the western Arabs. For without an income and strength of arms, Muhammad's religion might have disappeared in the wake of other self-proclaimed prophets and their sects. After a slow start, Muhammad's raiders gained some successes and other Arabs converted to Islam and joined his horde. Despite misgivings and hostility from many of Medina's inhabitants, the activities of the Muslims inevitably embroiled that town in a war against Mecca. The first battle evolved from an unsuccessful razzia. In 624, 300 Muslims beat off 900 Meccans. The conflict had started with with a few single combats and ended with less than a hundred dead on both sides. The battle of Badr was the first notable victory of the Muslim forces, and was interpreted as a victory of faith over the unbelievers.

Within Medina, Muhammad consolidated his political position. Leading opponents were assassinated. Jews were expelled and massacred. Two Meccan attacks on Medina were repulsed and in 630, after Muhammad had assembled an unusually large force which overawed the city, the Muslims entered Mecca peacefully. Over the next years, Muhammad defeated rival tribes and towns, emerging as the most powerful man in Arabia. Undefeated tribes rallied to his side as allies. As Muhammad's strength grew, these tribes converted to Islam. Only those Arabs to the north, nearest to the Byzantine and Persian empires, remained aloof from the new enthusiasm that had seized their neighbours. A couple of years before his death in 632, Muhammad led an expeditionary force, said to be 30,000 strong, along the trade route to Iraq. It foreshadowed conquests beyond Arabia.

The Muslim forces that achieved the first victories of Islam were samll and unprofessional. Essentially they were raiders, used to attacking caravans and not prepared armies. Muhammad's supporters were towns-men from Mecca and Medina with Bedouin recruited from the interior.

Silver dish of the 5th century, showing King Bahram V on a lion hunt. Sasanid Persian weaponry and armour influenced steppe warriors such as the Huns and Turks, and later influenced the Arabs. Dish now in the British Museum, London.

Many were motivated by the prospect of booty, some by the desire of their leader to spread the new religion. The raiders and Bedouin rode horses. In large-scale confrontations, however, the majority of Muslim townsmen went into battle on foot. Camels were used mainly as pack-animals, although warriors sometimes rode them into battle but then dismounted. They do not appear to have been used in tactical formations like those of the Moors and rarely did warriors fight from their camel back. When battle was engaged, camels were usually left behind in camp where they were hobbled to prevent them from being easily rustled away by enemy raiders. The number of horses available to the Muslims was very small at first, but this grew with every victory.

Alongside the more prosperous Muslims fought their slaves. Inspired by the egalitarianism of Islam, these slaves fought particularly well. According to tradition, the first Muslim killed in battle was a black slave called Mihja. Another slave, a Persian, was credited with suggesting the digging of a ditch around Medina that saved the town from the Meccans. But aside from the promise of their new faith, slaves fought effectively in battle for other reasons. On the positive side, success in combat could bring a slave renown, promotion, favours, perhaps even liberty if he saved his master's life. On one occasion, later in the 7th century, a commander urged his massed levies of slaves onwards with the words, 'The slave who fights is free.' So encouraged, observers were astonished at the vigour of the slaves as they gained victory. Fighting also gave a slave the opportunity to prove himself a man of worth in his own right. On the negative side, fear of defeat and death, as well as fear of punishment if they did not fight well, instilled many slaves with greater martial energy. Such considerations seem to have overcome any doubts that their masters may have had in arming a potentially hostile group of men. Besides, at the beginning of their struggle for survival, Muhammad and his followers were desperate for any able-bodied recruits. Their slaves, particularly the physically strong agricultural workers, could often endure the harsh conditions of campaign better than their town-bred masters.

Some slaves rose to prominence through their efforts in battle. Wahshī was a black Ethiopian highly skilled at spear throwing. At first he was employed by his master, an opponent of Muhammad, to kill the Prophet's uncle. This he achieved in battle and thus obtained his liberty. When Mecca was taken by the Muslims, Wahshī fled to Tā'if. There, he fell in with a group of citizens who converted to Islam. He attempted to obtain forgiveness from Muhammad but was dismissed. He turned to drink and was conspicuous for wearing bright red clothes. At the battle of Yamāma, the Ethiopian seized a chance to redeem himself. Fighting with the Muslims, he charged fearlessly towards the enemy commander and struck him dead, thus saving Islam from its chief 'false prophet'. 'I killed the best of men after Muhammad,' Wahshī claimed in later life, 'and then the worst of them.' Eventually, his drinking killed him. Such slave warriors were not professional soldiers in the sense of the military slaves acquired and trained by Muslim dynasties, like the Egyptian Mamlûks, in later centuries. The systematic raising of elite corps of professional slave warriors did not become institutionalised until the 9th century. Until that time slaves only fought as occasional retainers, defending their masters in battle, much like medieval European serfs. The best that could be said of them was encapsulated by an Arabic poet thus

'One obedient slave is better
than three hundred sons.
For the latter desire their father's death,
the former his master's glory.'

The death of the Prophet could well have been the end of Islam had not a string of remarkably strong and determined men taken over leadership of the religion and the Arabs. These leading disciples of Muhammad were known as caliphs. Not suprisingly, the main task the first caliph, Abū Bakr, had to face on his succession was to maintain the unity of the Arabs. Encouraged by the success of Muhammad, 'false prophets' sprung up throughout the country. By calling themselves 'prophets', these men hoped

Sasanid iron sword with silver scabbard from the 6th or 7th centuries. These blades were adopted by the conquering Muslim armies of Arabia. In the British Museum, London.

to detach themselves from the relentless inter-tribal suspicions and rivalries that had dogged previous attempts at greater centralisation of power. A spiritual man was seen to be above politics, unaligned to any faction, therefore only he could be a truly unbiased ruler of several tribes. Whether this had lain intentionally behind Muhammad's rise to power is uncertain, but it was a fundamental factor in his triumph. The elimination of competition by Caliph Abū Bakr in the war of the Ridda established more potently than ever before the Arabs as a single force. Under the reign of the Caliph 'Umar, this energy was directed against foreign non-Muslims. With the invasion of Mesopotamia, Palestine and Syria, the *Jihad* – or Holy War – was carried onto alien territory. Internal peace and external conquest profoundly transformed the Arabs. From an array of feuding tribes they had become a nation, a major Mediterranean power.

Much has been made of the belief that it was the strength of their faith that brought the Muslims so many spectacular victories. Certainly, today in the Middle East, the militancy of fundamentalist Muslim groups causes their more liberal neighbours to shudder as they witness the willingness of the hardliners to die for their beliefs. It can be argued, however, that such religious zeal has the authority of over a thousand years of established worship: and is frequently associated with fervent nationalism. The religion of the first caliphs was only a few decades old and must still have been widely misinterpreted and confused with other monotheistic faiths in the region. Such a newcomer to the philosophies of the Middle East would not have had the weight of tradition needed to impress many Arabs. That said, the doctrines of Jihad did promise a place in heaven to any warrior who died for Islam. This paradise was conceived as a wonderful garden running with cool streams. For a desert nomad, vulnerable to the superstitions and visions of afterlife that enveloped most people at this time, such a heaven was highly attractive. Warriors thus fearless of death would indeed have made an invincible force. And yet the West had its own spiritual promise for faithful warriors. Christianity offered its defenders an equally comforting afterlife. Even those Germans still motivated by pagan beliefs knew that to die fighting meant ascension to the glorious halls of their War Gods. But it was only the most religion-obsessed minds on all sides that truly believed such images: only a core of warrior mystics. The majority of men knew it was better to survive than be killed. Such commonsense cannot have been any less prevalent among rank and file Muslims.

Both Islam and Christianity preached the basic tenet that it was wrong to kill a man, but made an exception when that man was an infidel and opposed to one's own religion. The Jihad had its parallel in Christianity with the just wars condoned by Saint Augustine, and the crusades of later centuries. Yet Islam is still regarded as a stronger motivating force than the faith of the Byzantines or the Franks. This cannot be true, and is largely the result of Western cynicism regarding a belief close to hand, while maintaining a certain respect for a mysterious system of faith. The primary motivating force among the majority of Arab warriors was the same as that which stimulated medieval crusaders and has always excited soldiers. The prospect of booty and the licensing of outrageous behaviour. The success of the early Muslims simply encouraged many more Arabs to clamber on the wagon of ruthless enterprise. It was a campaign of conquest that made nomads rich beyond their own meagre pastoralism and transformed merchants into dynastic imperial governors. That solid material ambition underpinned much of the Muslim conquest is revealed even by Muhammad. When the Prophet placed Amr ibn al-As, the future conqueror of Egypt, in command of some warriors, he announced, 'May God keep you safe and bring you much booty.' Amr rejoined, 'I did not become a Muslim for the sake of wealth, but for the sake of submission to God.' To which the Prophet concluded, 'Honest wealth is good for an honest man.'

The most realistic and effective aspect of Islam in its conquest of half the Mediterranean world was its tolerance of Christians and Jews. Whenever subjugated by the Muslims, they were treated with respect and allowed to continue as before. For they were all People of the Book, sharing the same religious old Testament background. Such a policy meant that Christian and Jewish populations were far less hostile to the invaders than they might have been. To them it did not really matter whether their overlords were Byzantine, Persian or Arab. The Muslims only offered their adversaries 'conversion or the sword' when they were worshippers of idols or many gods. As there were few such cults around the Mediterranean, the Muslims found themselves in charge of increasing numbers of 'protected groups' or dhimmī. These People of the Book were allowed to practise their own faith in return for a regular protection payment to their conquerors. The Muslims frequently left economies to continue as before and simply lived off the taxes, thus leaving them independent, not tied to new estates. In this way, the Muslim forces were constantly funded and free to move on.

In Christian Europe, the doctrine of chivalry evolved to curb the excesses of war. Similarly, the Jihad incorporated a code of military conduct. But unlike chivalry, which was an unwritten code emerging from a general Christian aristocratic regard for honourable decency, the rules of Jihad were actually inscribed in works on Islamic law. The killing of women, children and old men was forbidden, unless they fought against Muslims. The wanton destruction of crops was discouraged. Prisoners converted to Islam were not to be killed. Other prisoners should not be tortured to death or mutilated, although they could be executed. Grants of safe-conduct and quarter must be upheld. Similarly, peace treaties and armistice agreements could be entered into with non-Muslims. Before war was embarked upon, a summons to Islam must have been issued to the enemy state. Like the vague humanity of chivalry, such a code was frequently broken in the heat of battle. In addition, there were so many differing interpretations of Islamic law that outright contradictions of many of the above measures were justified by a variety of sects.

Charles Martel, called 'the Hammer' by later historians, smashes an Arab force near Tours in AD 732. From Ward Lock's *Illustrated History of the World*, 1885.

For centuries, the Sasanid Persian Empire had been the Roman Empire's principal Eastern enemy. In the early 7th century, both forces were exhausted and recovering from their costly conflicts. On top of this, the Sasanid dynasty was politically unsteady and vulnerable to a sudden, unexpectedly powerful thrust from the south. But the Persians were no easy target: indeed, in their initial contact with the Muslims they severely defeated the invaders. The reluctance of the Arabs to give up the struggle triumphed, however, and in the end they captured a series of ancient capitals. The Barbaric behaviour of the victorious nomads shocked the more refined Persians. The Arabs tore up priceless carpets studded with jewels and shared them among each other. Dogs were fed off gold platters and luxurious aromatic substances were mistaken for food spices and tipped into soups. As the Persian Empire quickly crumbled, Arab forces launched attacks on Byzantine Palestine and Syria. With a sandstorm blowing in their enemy's faces, the Muslims tore apart a Byzantine army at the second battle of Yarmuk. Aided by the passivity of the native population the Arabs soon dominated both provinces. In 638, Muslims occupied Jerusalem. A year later, they invaded Egypt and threw out the Byzantines. This was particularly galling for the Empire as it had just expended a great deal of effort in recapturing the land from the Persians.

From their campaigns against the Persians and the Byzantines, the Arabs gained much. Their primitive warfare of enthusiasm aided by fortune was transformed into a more sophisticated system of war through acquisition and adaption. Horses had been rare amongst the Muslims before they left Arabia, but as they conquered the lands of the Persian and Byzantine empires, they acquired the finest horses of the East. The Syrian-Arab crossbreed combined weight with strength and became a vital weapon in further Islamic expansion. So much so did the Arabs take to horses that the small force of 4,000 that invaded Egypt in 639 was almost exclusively made up of horse-warriors. Among these riders the stirrup was known but was largely disdained as a sign of weakness. Only later did it become a generally accepted device. Camels and mules were still ridden while on the march to save the horses for battle.

In Arabia, the Muslims had also been poor in arms and armour. From the Byzantines and Persians, the Arabs looted mail and scale armour and witnessed the effective use of heavy cavalry so protected. Arab nobles were greatly impressed by their Sasanid counterparts clad entirely in iron. Veils of mail covering their faces gave them a dramatic appearance; while strips of iron were fastened on to their mail shirts around their torso; and yet more mail or scale armour protected their horses. Ammianus referred to earlier warriors so encased as looking 'not like men, but statues polished by the hand of Praxiteles'. Perhaps, however, leading Muslims rejected such a display as decadent. Chroniclers commented on the victorious entry of the Muslims into their cities as impressively unshowy compared to the Byzantines or Persians. This may have been because the majority of Arabs wore their mail shirts between layers of clothing: similarly, helmets were swathed in turbans. In the case of mail, covering it with linen may have been intended to deflect the direct rays of the sun, to prevent it from heating the bare metal to an unbearable condition.

Of course, not all Muslim warriors wore armour. Frequent injections of poor nomadic tribesmen meant that there were alway a great many lightly clad horsemen in all Muslim armies. This contributed to the preference of many Muslim commanders for campaigns that were a series of raids rather than pitched battles. That said, there does appear to have been a strong strain of Germanic-like chivalry in Arab warfare: a need for direct confrontation. For though the Arabs employed the composite bow as a matter of necessity, particularly when fighting against Central Asian Turks, the horse-archer did not play an overwhelming role in early Muslim warfare. Foot archers were employed to great effect but much mounted fighting was still carried out with sword and spear. Single combat was favoured and many battles were decided by hand-to-hand fighting. In the civil wars of 657, a duel between two Arab champions was recorded. Both Abbās ibn Rabiah and Irar ibn Adham dismounted to confront each other. The warriors wore coats of mail. Abbās' mail covered his head and was so long – being intended for horseback – that he had to tuck part of it into his belt. In fact, so completely protected were they by their mail that their sword blows proved fruitless. Becoming tired and desperate, Abbās suddenly noticed a gap in Irar's armour. He tore this aside with one hand and then plunged his sword into his opponent's naked chest. Irar fell dying. In later centuries heavily armoured horse-archers became the regular core of most Arab armies. The early 10th century chronicler al-Tabarī lists the following essential arms and armour for a warrior: mail, breastplate, helmet, leg-guards, arm-guards, horse armour, lance, small shield, sword, mace, battle-axe, quiver of thirty arrows, bowcase with two bows and two spare bow strings. Such a 'tank' was clearly descended from the Byzantine and Sasanid *clibanarii*, so named after the Greek word for 'oven' – obviously how many a soldier felt!

Inevitably, the continued success of the Muslims brought great strains to their unity. Civil war broke out and for a few decades their conquests faltered. By the beginning of the 8th century, however, the whole of north Africa had fallen to the Muslims. Like other warriors before them, the temptation to cross a strip of sea just eighteen miles wide and pass from continent to continent proved overwhelming. In the town of Ceuta, opposite Gibraltar, they found themselves an ally. Count Julian, perhaps a Byzantine exiled from Spain or a disaffected Visigoth, demonstrated how easy it was to tap the wealth of Romano-Goth Iberia. Accompanied by Muslims, his men raided the southern-most tip of the peninsula. Thus encouraged, a year later in 711, a force of 7,000 warriors commanded by a Berber called Tāriq, set sail in ships provided by Count Julian. For ever after, their landing place has been called Gibraltar, *Jabel Tāriq*, 'the mountain of Tāriq'. The army consisted mostly of Berbers, nomads of the Sahara who had converted to Islam and provided some of the fiercest warriors of the Arab invasions.

Racked by conflicts over succession, the Visigoth kingdom of Spain was unable to field a united front. After the Muslims had established themselves and received reinforcements, they were finally confronted by the Visigoth King Roderick somewhere north of the salt-lake of Janda. The Berbers had rustled many horses from local farms and so met the Iberian Germans on horseback. Both sides fought with swords and spears. Gangs of noble horse-warriors were supported by bands of foot-soldiers. The Berbers were veteran warriors of the Muslim African campaigns and fared well against the reluctant farmers and serfs desperately assembled as an army by Goth landlords. Roderick had already suffered from crippling desertions on his way south from Toledo. And now, as the Berbers charged forward, swathed

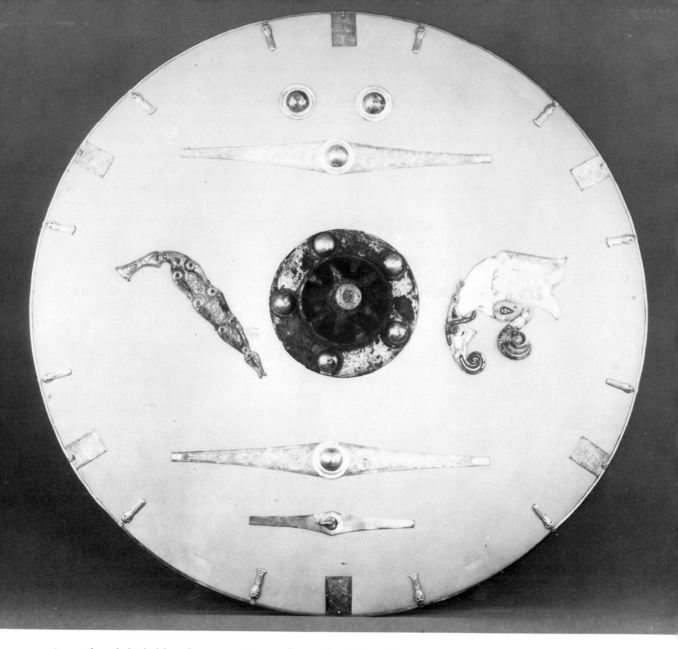

in mail and dark blue face-covering turbans, the Visigoth ranks shuddered and broke. Roderick and his retainers were killed.

The Muslim advance towards the Visigoth capital of Toledo in central Spain was rapid. The Jewish and Byzantine inhabitants of the region made no pretence of resistance. They had suffered much under the oppressive regime of the Goths and were happy to exchange it for the less intolerant rule of Islam. Indeed, the Jews, with north African allies, had organised an abortive revolt against the Visigoths in the last years of the previous century and savage massacres of the Jews had followed. Local Visigoth warlords did, of course, oppose the invaders but there was no central co-ordination and their unity had long been shattered by dynastic rivalry.

Some Goths even helped the Arabs in the hope of future political preferment. The Visigoth kingdom was spent, and in the face of a determined invader, it fell apart. Over the next few years, many more Arab warriors arrived and key cities were subdued. As with previous Barbarian invasions, not every community in a country as vast as Spain could be said to be under direct Arab control, but by 716 the conquest was complete and al-Andalus, or Andalusia, emerged as the first European province of the Muslim Empire.

Throughout their conquests, the Muslims were aided by the internal exhaustion and collapse of their chief adversaries. The Sasanids, Byzantines and Visigoths were all caught at their least dynamic. With the Muslim invasion of southern France, however, they came against a far more vigorous opponent, though this was not immediately apparent. For on the surface, if the inhabitants of France had depended on their royal family to protect them there would be Islamic palaces in Aquitaine today to equal the Alhambra. The Merovingian dynasty of Franks had kept a firm grip on the lands of Gaul for two centuries but was now in decline. Real power was held by men behind the throne, the Mayors of the Palace. This role, of defender and maintainer of the state, was assumed by the Arnulfing dynasty and was handed from father to son. From this family emerged the Carolingian monarchs.

At the time of the first Arab raids into southern France it was the illegitimate son of one of these mayors who took command in the crisis – Charles Martel. The principal landholder in north France and western Germany, Martel had one major rival – Eudo – warlord of Aquitaine. When news reached Charles of substantial Muslim conquests in and around Narbonne he could see that Eudo had his hands full and monitored the outcome with great interest. As the Arabs consolidated their position, Eudo struck back and defeated them soundly, killing their commander. But relentless as ever, the Muslims sent further expeditionary forces via the Rhone valley. For over a decade the Arab raiders plundered the rich lands of Provence until finally, in 732, the Arabs embarked on their second large scale invasion and crossed the Pyrenees. This time, Eudo was beaten and pursued into central France. Fearing an attack on his own lands, though more interested in the outcome of a victory achieved on his rival's territory, Charles Martel seized the opportunity of Eudo's rout and marched south. Joining remnants of Eudo's army just south of Tours, Charles drew up his warriors in defence of this rich religious centre. An alternative tradition, recorded by Fredegar, relates that Eudo and Charles had already clashed in several border incidents. Worsted by Charles' raiders, Eudo then invited the Arabs to join him in an attack on Martel. Therefore, in the battle that followed, Christians fought alongside Muslims against the Franks of northern France.

For a week, both forces sent raiders against each other: testing their strength. This delay allowed the Arab commander, 'Abd al-Rahmān al-

Ghāfiqī, to secure the passage of his wagons laden with booty back to safer zones. Why Charles did not employ the advantage of surprise to attack his foes immediately is unknown. According to Fredegar he did, but other records give time in which the Arabs were allowed to save their goods and prepare for battle. This week of waiting would also have allowed the Franks to ride through the district and gather local men to fight alongside the professional warriors loyal to Charles. When battle was finally begun, tradition has it that the majority of Franks fought on foot, shoulder to shoulder, in an impenetrable iron phalanx of shields and spears. This was certainly true of the hastily assembled farmhands and citizens, who could do little else but fight on foot. Many of the aristocratic retainers of the leading Frank nobles, however, would have remained on their horses in the hope of rapidly exploiting weaknesses amongst the enemy.

As a force of raiders the Muslims must have been largely mounted, and it makes sense that it was they who opened the battle. (Though here again, Fredegar says that it was Charles who came upon them 'like a mighty man of war'.) Such a large invasion force must have included many foot-soldiers as well, for these were still an important element of Arab warfare. Therefore, it is likely that crowds of Berbers, Arabs, recently recruited Christians and Jews, all fought side by side in a phalanx of sword and spear carriers to equal that of the Franks. There were more archers among the Arabs than the Franks, but hails of arrows were probably not a determining feature. Also, the traditional picture of lightly clad Arab horsemen hurling themselves against heavily armoured Frank foot-soldiers must be discounted. Instead it is more likely that the Muslims, veteran raiders and well supplied with looted arms from recently defeated Frank adversaries, fielded more men clad in mail and brandishing swords than the poorly equipped levies of Charles Martel.

The fighting was fierce, lasting until nightfall. Arab and Frank horsemen probably came to blows first, as the most noble horse-warriors hoped to obtain victory quickly with an initial display of daring and skill. Once exhausted, they then fell back amidst their rows of foot-soldiers. As the battle progressed, groups of warriors advanced and entrapped isolated horsemen. Prodding them with their spears, pushing them off their horses, forcing blades through gaps in their mail and ripping off anything of value. It was a battle of muscle and endurance; swords bashed against shields and spears pierced bodies. Beneath their mail many of the chief warriors suffered only battering and bruises. Blows to their spirit rather than their bodies. It was the unprotected and unprepared peasant levies who were slashed and gored, trampled and crushed, and it was these men who quit the battlefield first if suffering visibly-great losses. Indeed, considering the more professional quality of the Muslim warriors it is remarkable that the Arabs did not gain another victory. But, on returning to their camps, the Muslims learned that their commander was dead and the next day they retreated before the weary but triumphant Franks.

An early portrait of Charlemagne and his wife. Beneath is his signature from a document of AD 775. A late 19th century engraving from a Carolingian manuscript of between AD 817 and 823, now preserved at the monastery of St Paul in Carinthia, Austria.

Signum KRS Ecclesiae Longobardimensis

At first, the Muslims would have seen their defeat near Tours as just a temporary setback in the overall tide of Islam. But as time passed, it became clear that this was to be the furthest north into Europe the Arabs would ever penetrate. From then on, Charles Martel kept up a constant pressure on the Muslim raiders and slowly the Franks expelled them from their recent conquests north of the Pyrenees, eventually recapturing Narbonne. The tide had turned. The determination of the Franks outweighed that of the Arabs. Mass raiding north of the Pyrenees had become unprofitable, but the western reaction went further. In the mountains of north-west Spain, Visigoth warlords held out against the Muslims. From this kingdom of the Asturias sprung the warriors of the *Reconquista*. A crusader project that obsessed Christian Spain for the whole of the Middle Ages, and piece by piece recaptured the land. In the meantime, through his victory against the Muslims, Charles Martel had spread his dominion over most of southern France. The Arnulfings had risen in power and reputation to such a degree that Martel's son, Pepin III, felt confident enough to end the pretence of the Merovingians and place himself upon the throne. The Carolingians were possessed with all the energy of a new dynasty and pursued several expansionist campaigns while, in contrast, the dynamism of the Muslims was being drained by internal dispute. A revolt by the Berbers weakened the hold of the Arabs over Spain and allowed further Christian resurgence. Nevertheless, later Arab consolidation maintained the country as a principal Muslim power, and for the next few centuries the Franks and Arabs remained uneasy neighbours.

With half the old Roman Empire absorbed by followers of a new religion and culture, and the other half occupied largely by Germanic kingdoms, it seems that the Ancient World had definitely come to an end – this period is generally referred to as the Early Middle Ages – and yet this transition from era to era was far from sharply defined. Certainly the ancient unity of the Roman Empire, centred around the Mediterranean, seems to have been ripped in half. Yet this was a cultural and political division, not an economic one. Trade between all ports around the Mediterranean was vital to each ruling hierarchy and continued as before. Christian, Jewish and Muslim merchants had no qualms about dealing with each other, even though their lords were at war. Frequent punitive raids and the activities of unchecked pirates lessened the quantity of this trade, but where there was a good chance of some return on a trip to a far flung country, sailors and merchants could always be found to undertake it. Culturally and politically, Islam may have appeared alien to Christian, Graeco-Roman Europe but even here one is discussing its essence rather than the day-to-day reality. Frequently, Muslim governors were happy to see the old Roman-Byzantine bureaucracy, economy and religions they inherited carry on as before. The major impetus for the increased conversion to Islam among the majority of inhabitants in the conquered territories of the Near East, Africa and Spain was simply that they could advance further socially if they adopted the state religion.

In 8th century Europe, the links between the Ancient and Medieval worlds were maintained as often as they were broken. The Byzantine state was still officially and legally recognised as the legitimate Roman Empire. A calculated insult, often employed by the Franks, was to address the Byzantine ruler as Emperor of the Greeks and not Emperor of the Romans. Not just an heir to Imperial glory, Byzantium remained an energetic force in Eastern Europe for centuries to come. In 718, the Emperor Leo so decisively defeated the Arabs outside Constantinople that they never again tried to invade Europe via the Balkans. As regards the Germanic kingdoms of Italy and France, the determination of the northern invaders to maintain a degree of Latin civilisation – merely exchanging the authority of Roman land-owners for that of German landlords – has already been stated. The wars that followed the Barbarian invasions of the 5th century were no more disruptive than the Roman civil wars of earlier centuries. Warlords had always governed semi-autonomously throughout southern Europe and would continue to do so, whether it be under the guise of the Roman Empire or more nakedly in the Latinised kingdoms of the Germans. Therefore, to an observer unbiased by false historical divisions, early medieval Europe sustained a character similar to that of the late Roman Empire. Crucial to this continuity was the institution of Christianity which, having survived and prospered throughout virtually the entire history of the Roman Empire, was a powerful link with the Ancient World: but the most celebrated evocation of the continuing presence of the old Western Empire was yet to come.

Outside the Christian bastion of Constantinople, the Catholic faith was championed by the Roman Papacy, which was developing its political strength and status in central Italy. It was a minor crisis in this growth that led to the spectacle of a Germanic king assuming the discarded mantle of Western Roman Emperor. All previous Germanic warlords had felt it unnecessary to fill the throne vacated years before by Romulus Augustulus, preferring the sham of allegiance to the Eastern Emperor. In the year 800, however, Pope Leo III was in dire trouble with the citizens of Rome. Narrowly escaping assassination, he had been slashed across the face by a gang of rivals and forced to flee to Germany. Receiving no help from the Eastern Empire, he wrote to the Carolingian King of the Franks and urged him to come to his rescue. Charlemagne arrived in Rome, put down the revolt, and secured the position of the Pope. In return, Leo insisted that a king of the Franks and the Lombards, with a domain covering Gaul, Germany and northern Italy, should have his imperial status recognised. Reluctant to spoil his friendly relations with the Emperor of the East, Charlemagne nevertheless agreed to be crowned Emperor and Augustus. The title of Holy Roman Emperor was not actually adopted until many centuries later, by the Germans in 1254, but in the minds of many, the Western Roman Empire had been dramatically resurrected. As one contemporary chronicler exclaimed 'He who ordains the fate of kingdoms and the march of centuries – the all-powerful Disposer of events – having destroyed one extraordinary image, that of the Romans, then raises up among the Franks the golden head of a second image, equally remarkable, in the person of Charlemagne.'

The Carolingian domain was not a Mediterranean-bound Empire, its heart had shifted to the Rhineland, but it did occupy many of the provinces once held by the Caesars. With such vast lands under its control, it was the strongest power-base in Western Europe. In the whole continent, it was second only in authority to the Byzantine Empire. As officially acknowledged 'Defender of the Church' by the Papacy, the Carolingian dynasty was perceived as a preserver of the Roman Christian tradition. As a result its wars of expansion into central Europe and its wars of defence against raiders, were considered battles against Barbarians. These new Barbarians were Avars, Slavs, Magyars and Northmen – the Vikings. They were no more Barbaric than the Carolingian warriors that slaughtered them: but they were pagan outsiders, while the Franks managed – in the eyes of western history – to be regarded as the holy agents of civilisation.

The wolves of Wodan

'I am a man alone,' wrote a warrior of the Dark Ages. 'As I recall the slaughter of my comrades, there is no one I can open my heart to. The man mindful of his reputation does not reveal his sadness. Ever since I buried my lord, ever since I lost my companions, I must mourn alone. Now I have left my home land, I sail the icy seas in search of a new lord. A generous giver of gold. A lord who will welcome me into his drinking-hall and divert me from my grief.

'With no friends to assist me, I remind myself of the hall full of retainers. The receiving of treasures from my lord after the feast. My youth. I remember resting my head and hands upon the knee of my lord and pledging my loyalty. Then I awake from my thoughts and see the dark waves lashing around me. The hail and snow beating down. I wish all the more to see my warrior friends, to be welcomed with song. But again these images are soon gone. It is little wonder that my spirit is darkened by the fate of man. How brave warriors, one by one, must leave the mead-hall.

'A man cannot be wise until he has endured the winters of his life. A wise man must be patient. Not easy to anger, nor loose of speech. Neither rash nor unreliable in battle. He should not lack courage, nor be greedy for plunder. He should never boast actions before he can achieve them. He must hold back his promises until he has thought them through and has no doubt. A wise man must contemplate destruction. For now, ancient walls are decaying, ravaged by wind and frost. Grand buildings, the work of giants, stand deserted. The wine-halls crumble. All the proud lords and their warriors lie dead. Falling in battle, one was carried over the sea by a raven: another was devoured by a wolf: and one was buried by his heart-broken retainer.

'So he who thinks deep about destruction and the battles of the past cannot fail to ask 'Where now is the war-horse? Where is the warrior clad in mail? Where the giver of gold and feasts? Where is the glory of my lord?' These days are long gone. All that remains is a monument carved with serpents. Where once warriors were laid down by a hail of ash-spears, now a storm of sleet batters their stone. Winter howls and the hardship of life fills men. Wealth is fleeting, comrades are fleeting. Man is transient. I wander through a wilderness.'

This passage, a prose rendering of an Anglo-Saxon poem commonly called *The Wanderer*, is a moving insight to the mind of the professional warrior. Without a lord, a warrior could not function. From a lord came all the wealth – material and emotional – that sustained a man in his martial status. With a loyalty proclaimed to one lord, on his death the faithful warrior became an exile. A masterless wanderer. It was far better that he should die in battle alongside his lord, rather than endure survival. Such a close, mutually dependent relationship was recorded by Tacitus in his 1st century description of the German tribes, and was still present a thousand years later in Germanic literature. It was the core around which all the honour and nobility of the medieval hero was constructed.

Throughout *The Wanderer*, loyalty is implicit in the warrior's sense of loss and aimlessness. In the third paragraph the author then lists other qualities desirable in retainers. But what did the warrior expect from his master? How could a warlord preserve his status as a man of supreme power? The first requirement for the maintenance of power throughout the first millennium was – as it always has been – wealth. With food, shelter, weapons, armour, horses and money, a man could gather around him a formidable bodyguard. For many landlords, the possession of wealth was enough to sustain power. However, for warriors to fight to the death for a lord, many demanded attributes in their leader that were of a physical and moral character. Retainers thrived on personal respect for their master. Such renown was recorded by chroniclers and if sufficiently outstanding would ensure the everlasting fame of the lord as well as his closest supporters. Being a man of respect was almost as potent as being a man of wealth. Courage, physical strength, skill in handling weapons, all earned the respect of other men. Important too was wisdom: the intelligence to command men effectively in battle, the wit to handle negotiations and peacetime government.

After such essential features, less weighty talents impressed many a warband. Nordic sagas are particularly full of such skills. The Norwegian warlord Olaf Tryggvason was renowned for juggling three daggers at once, catching them always by the hilts. He was able to walk from oar to oar alongside the outside of his longboat while the men were rowing. Such talents recall the circus antics of the Goth king Totila before the battle of Taginae in 552. Neither chieftains' followers were dismayed or embarrassed by such displays: they would have admired their leaders all the more. And yet, could one imagine a Roman general encouraging the respect of his men by juggling swords in the air? There seems to have been a very definite division between the bounds of decorum expected from leaders of Mediterranean soldiers and those of Germanic warriors. Indeed, the further north one goes, the less were the limits of dignity. Running, rowing, skiing and swimming were all noble demonstrations of prowess among the Scandinavians. They even considered it worthy to make their own weapons. They were proud of their technical skills and hence the inclusion of many details of weapon manufacture in nordic literature. Similarly, the skilled use of the bow, a weapon left to the lowest classes of foot-soldiers amongst the majority of Germans, was a matter of vital concern between two Norwegian kings debating their relative merits in the *Heimskringla saga*. However, such a use of the bow was confined to sport and hunting, so that when it came to battle, the spear and sword remained the primary weapons of the aristocrat. As far as Scandinavian nobles were concerned, the only pursuits that were considered unseemly for men of their rank were those skills arising from commerce and farming. Such a prejudice against the mastery of earning a living outside the bounds of pillaged or inherited wealth continued amongst aristocracy throughout the Middle Ages and after.

Aside from protecting their lords, faithful warriors were expected to be their avengers. Regardless of their Christianity, revenge was a strong motivating force among Germanic warriors, and vendettas frequently sparked off full scale campaigns. Paul the Deacon, in his 8th century *History of the Lombards*, records the private vengeance one servant undertook for the killing of his master. On an Easter Sunday, this man, a dwarf, hid himself in the font of a baptistry. When the betrayer of his lord passed through the church, the dwarf suddenly emerged and cut off the warrior's head. He himself was quickly killed but through such an action he had

Fierce carved head from the stem-post of a 4th or 5th century Danish ship found in the River Scheldt in Belgium; evidence of the presence of nordic pirates in the North Sea long before what we now know as the Viking Age. Now in the British Museum, London.

revived the honour of his lord as well as ending the humiliation of outliving him. Honour in battle is best exemplified by another Anglo-Saxon poem. In *The Battle of Maldon*, written shortly after the event, many of the fine qualities of the warrior-retainer (as mentioned above) are featured. Faults are also made plain. The Battle of Maldon took place in the south-east of England in 991. It was one of countless bloody encounters with Viking raiders in Anglo-Saxon Britain and Carolingian France throughout the 9th and 10th centuries. On this occasion, the Northmen had sailed through the Blackwater estuary in East Anglia and camped on the little island of Northey.

The poetic account of the Battle of Maldon begins with Byrhtnoth, a great English lord, commanding his warriors to dismount and advance into battle on foot. We can assume that this order only applied to his personal retinue of leading warriors. Such a decision may well have been due to the marshy terrain around the Blackwater, making effective riding impossible. Also, it seems that Byrhtnoth wished to fight a defensive battle and a dismounted band of warriors were far steadier when receiving attacks. Certainly, on this occasion, the Vikings were without horses themselves and so Byrhtnoth simply confronted them on equal terms. It has been suggested that Anglo-Saxon warfare may have been less ready to use horses and that the English were primarily foot-soldiers, like the early Franks. But with a Celtic and Roman legacy, as well as the Germanic noble status attached to horsemanship, it seems more than likely that – like any continental army – Anglo-Saxons did use horses in battle when taking the offensive and pursuing a broken enemy.

As the Anglo-Saxon warriors assembled under Byrhtnoth's orders, one young noble let his prized hunting hawk fly from his wrist. A symbolic act appreciated by the poet. Once arrayed in their position of battle, Byrhtnoth dismounted and joined his finest warriors in the shield-wall. A landlord of considerable standing, it has been estimated that Byrhtnoth was a white-haired man of about sixty. The confrontation with the Danish raiders opened with an exchange of insults. The Viking spokesmen announced that they would be happy to leave the area in return for a tribute of gold. Greatly offended, Byrhtnoth, or more likely an official messenger – a herald – shouted back, 'Listen pirates, the only tribute we shall send you is one of spear-points and veteran sword-edge. We are the guardians of our people, our land and our King. It is the heathen who shall fall.' Byrhtnoth and his warriors then strode towards the edge of the river bank. Both sides glared at each other across the water. A few arrows were let fly. Some Danes endeavoured to use a ford but the East Saxons, men of Essex, stoutly prevented them.

Wearying of the stalemate, the Vikings asked if they could have permission to cross the ford and thus begin the battle. Somewhat over-confidently, according to the poet, Byrhtnoth allowed the enemy to cross over onto the mainland. At first, such a decision appears to have a ring

'Across the whale's domain'. Viking seafarers travelled far in their search for plunder. A late 19th century engraving.

of Germanic chivalry about it, but if refused a battle the Danes would
simply have sailed off, and ravaged some other part of the coast which was
unprotected. At least the Anglo-Saxons had the chance to finish off the
Viking menace there and then. The Danes, called by the poet the wolves of
Wodan, God of War, waded across the ford with their lime-wood shields
and weapons held high. The Anglo-Saxons drew themselves up in a closely
packed crowd, fronted by shield-carrying warriors, ready for the Viking
onslaught.

When the warriors clashed, shouts and screams ripped across the
countryside. Case-hardened spears were thrown. Bows were busy. In close
combat, sword and spear slashed and stabbed. The majority of Anglo-Saxon
soldiers were local levies and poorly equipped. Their thick leather jackets,
if they possessed them, would have afforded little protection against the
professional weaponry of the Vikings, collected over many raids. The
Anglo-Saxon nobles and their retainers were clad in mail and parried sword

blows with their metal-strengthened shields. From these ranks came the stiffest resistance. One Dane, gripping his shield and spear, closed in on Byrhtnoth. The Viking threw his weapon and wounded the Saxon lord. According to the text, the Viking's weapon was a 'southern spear', that is made in a country to the south of Scandinavia and England, which must mean France. Elsewhere, in the struggle over the ford, there is mention of a Frankish spear, *francan*. It is unlikely that this was the early Frankish *angon*, but it may well have possessed the wing-like projections from its socket, supposedly characteristic of Frankish spears. After being pierced by the spear, Byrhtnoth is said to have broken the shaft with the edge of his shield. The Anglo-Saxon lord then threw one spear which passed through the Viking's neck and another that slit open his mail. Byrhtnoth laughed and thanked God for his good fortune. But no sooner had he dealt with one enemy than another wounded him, again with a thrown spear. A retainer next to him immediately withdrew the weapon from his lord's body and hurled it back, striking the Dane. Yet another Viking advanced on the Saxon leader, this time intending to steal the mail, rings and ornamented sword of the wounded man. Desperately, Byrhtnoth swung his broad, bright-edged sword at the robber. The Dane countered and slashed at the Saxon's arm, so that his gold-hilted sword fell to the ground. Beneath the frenzied blows of the enemy, the chieftain and his two closest retainers slumped to the ground.

With the death of their leader, some leading Saxons lost heart and took flight. One, in his panic, actually mounted the horse of his lord. Cowardice was bad enough, but this act was shocking: the poet notes that Byrhtnoth had frequently given gifts of horses to this same man. Other warriors joined the flight, forgetting their loyalty to their lord and the many gifts he had bestowed upon them. The words of a noble are recalled, warning Byrhtnoth that many warriors speak keenly of their courage but in battle they prove unequal to the stress. Those warriors that remained in battle intensified their struggle, determined to avenge their lord or die. Amongst the loyal retainers was a good-will hostage, obtained from a Northumbrian family, who fought with equal courage and used bow and arrow to inflict wounds upon the common enemy. Another bold warrior crashed through the shield-carrying Danes and plunged deep amongst the marauders.

The fighting was fierce. Shields were shattered, leaving warriors to punch their opponents with the remaining metal boss. Mail shirts rang as they were splintered in the fury. Soon many of the bravest retainers had fulfilled their vows of loyalty by dying alongside their lord. The majority of Anglo-Saxons had already fled, thinking the sight of their lord's horse galloping away meant that their leader was signalling a retreat. The battle was lost. Amidst the Saxon last stand, the author of the poem chose a veteran warrior to express words of heroic loyalty that would have impressed the poet's aristocratic audience. Said the old man, 'Heart must be braver, courage the bolder, mind the firmer, as our strength becomes lesser.

The siege of Paris in AD 885 was a bitterly fought campaign. The Vikings sailed their boats right up to the walls of the island city. From Guizot's *L'Histoire de France*, 1870.

Here lies our lord. A noble man, in blood and mud. Those who turn their back now will regret it forever. I am old. I will not leave here. I will lie beside my lord – the man I love most dearly.'

Within a couple of decades of this combat at Maldon, the Danes had conquered the whole of England and set their king upon the Anglo-Saxon throne. Elsewhere, on the continent, Danish Vikings had set up an independent state in northern France: while the Swedes had long established themselves in Russia: and the Norwegians ruled a north Atlantic dominion including Iceland and Greenland. The Scandinavian Vikings were the last pagan Northern people to descend on Europe and ravage established regimes. To Christian chroniclers, preservers of Roman Catholic civilisation, the first Vikings were devilish destroyers. They were Barbarians. Later like all Germanic invaders the Northmen (or Normans), with the responsibility of conquest became the hardiest defenders of the culture they had once violated. It was in their 'barbarous' state, however, that the Vikings accomplished some of their most characteristic military operations.

According to conventional histories, the impact of the Scandinavians was first noted around the year 800. Around this date, ferocious raids by Northmen on British monasteries and island communities were recorded. At the same time, the completion of a savage campaign against the Saxons in north-west Germany brought the Carolingians face to face with the warriors of Denmark. Viking raids soon followed. And yet, the belief that a new race of marauders had suddenly sprung out of Scandinavia is a false one. Scandinavian tribes had long been involved in the movements of Germanic Barbarians. Most of those German tribes that had invaded England in the 5th century came from Denmark. Many notable Barbarian confederations, such as the Goths, claimed to have originated in the lands of the Baltic. Nordic pirates had always been rife in the North Sea, using shallow-draught sea-going ships. The raids of the Vikings in the 9th and 10th centuries, were only the latest in a long tradition of sea-borne Scandinavian assaults. Gregory of Tours recorded a Danish raid, on the Frankish territory of King Theuderic in the early 6th century, which has all the characteristics of later Viking attacks. A Danish fleet ran ashore, captured some local inhabitants, loaded their ships with their booty and prepared to sail home. Theuderic reacted promptly, however, and beat the invaders in a naval battle, retrieving all the lost property.

Nevertheless, by the late 8th century, certain developments occurred which, in hindsight, gave the appearance of a sudden explosion of activity among the Scandinavians. They had perfected the design of their sea-going ships – sails were added to the power of their oars – and this led to an increase in the amount of piracy in the North Sea. Short trips across strips of sea or along familiar coastlines had always been possible, but now more extensive voyages could be undertaken. At the same time, in the period from 600 to 800, the Scandinavian language underwent a profound change that transformed it from a language similar to that of the Germans, to the south of them, to one that was specifically nordic. This, combined with the fact that the Scandinavians were still a pagan people, meant that they were now viewed by their neighbouring German kingdoms as an alien race. No longer did they share a language, culture, religion or common aims. While the Scandinavians still pursued a roving, scavaging way of life, their raids increasingly threatened the settled Germanic dynasties and Christian communities. The Scandinavians and Germans were no longer allies intent on sacking a Romanised Europe, for the Germans were now part of that Latin establishment, while the Scandinavians were still outsiders. Such an explanation of the Viking phenomonen in the west is far more convincing than the suggestion that there was a sudden population explosion in Scandinavia which forced its people outwards. Certainly, populations in Scandinavia were increasing, but this was common throughout Europe. In addition to the altered perspective in which the Scandinavians were regarded in the 9th and 10th centuries, it must be remembered that the Germanic chronicles which supposedly first record Viking raids against England and France were both compiled around the dates they mention. They are not accurate historical surveys over hundreds of years, and do not record regular occurrences before the time of their compilation. That there were no frequent raids by Scandinavian warbands on England and France before 800 is difficult to believe and contrary to archaeological evidence.

On one day in 782, Charlemagne had 4,500 Saxon prisioners massacred. It is little wonder then that Godfred, King of the Danes, watched with alarm as the Franks wiped out all opposition in north-west Germany and approached his territory. With Saxony subdued, the northern-most frontier of the Carolingians ran across the base of Jutland. At the heart of this Empire was a man who increasingly saw his wars of imperialist conquest as worthy crusades against the heathen Northerners. At first, relations between the two states was cordial. Danish chieftains were received at the court of Charlemagne despite the piratical activities of their fellow countrymen along the northern coast. To curb the Danish raids, Charlemagne strength-ened his coasts' guard and improved his fleet. Strongpoints were erected at all ports and at the mouths of rivers so that if any Vikings sailed into them, they could be bottled up by a special military task force. Similar defences were used in southern France and Italy against the Arabs. Indeed, it has been said that the strong coastal defences of the Franks were responsible for encouraging the Danes to venture a little further and turn to England in their search for softer targets.

By the first decade of the 9th century, the Carolingians had so far encroached on the Danes' sphere of influence that confrontation was inevitable. To prevent invasion, Godfred built an immense timber and earth rampart, called the Danework, which linked natural obstacles across Jutland from the North Sea to the Baltic. Then, in 810, he sent 200 ships into Frisian territory, recently acquired by the Carolingian Empire. The Danish seamen were unopposed and Godfred felt so confident of his powers that he

boasted that he would next invade Aachen, Charlemagne's capital. But, as Charlemagne prepared for the last campaign of his career, King Godfred was assassinated and the Danish threat melted away. A conflict had been established, however, and the two powers wrangled over the borderlands.

By the middle of the 9th century, Frisia was paying such regular protection money to the Danes that it could be considered Viking property. The Northmen therefore took their raids further afield, along the French coast and inland. There was very little the Carolingians could do. Following the death of Charlemagne, the old imperial realm had been torn by civil wars and was eventually divided into separate kingdoms, each more concerned about each other than with the raiders. Previously, the Danes had been content to run their shallow-draught boats up onto a beach, jump out, pillage a nearby community and leap back into their ships for a quick getaway. With an increase in the size of their fleets, experience of where they were going and a decrease in organised coastal defence, the Vikings grew more daring. The weakness of the Carolingian dominion encouraged an explosion of northern raiding. Once they landed, the Danes conducted small campaigns against the surrounding districts. They stole horses to ride inland and soon Viking armies were threatening major urban centres. The Franks were forced to pay massive tributes to the invaders. Even so, large stretches of land fell under direct Viking control. French peasants formed groups to ensure their own defence but were frequently crushed by Frank nobles in league with the Vikings. Many Franks hoped to ally themselves with the ascending power: the Carolingians were proving incapable of any concerted action. Often they had to resort to hiring Viking mercenaries to combat those Danes taking over their lands. At this time the efforts of Alfred the Great in England were reversing the flow of freebooters back to the continent for easy pickings.

Across both France and Germany, great cities went up in flames. Paris, situated on an island in the middle of the Seine, proved particularly attractive. It had been ravaged before but, in 885, a huge Danish army sailed upon it, probably intent on long-term conquest. With so many warriors crammed in to their dragon ships, the Danes decided to assault the city straightaway but, under the command of Count Eudes, the island fortress proved a tough nut to crack. As the Vikings clambered up their scaling ladders, clutching swords and axes, the Parisians poured boiling oil, wax and pitch upon them. The scalding liquid clung to the warriors and many, in their agony, tried to tear the burning hair from their heads. Unable to storm Paris immediately, the Danes settled in for a siege. As they endeavoured to cut the city off from the outside world, they constructed awesome engines. Massive battering rams of oak were raised onto roofed carriages having sixteen wheels. Large screens, capable of shielding four men, were covered with the skin of young bulls: holes were made in them through which burning arrows were fired. Several catapults hurled lumps of molten lead into the city.

The ingenuity of the Danes was matched by that of the Parisians. When the siege machines were brought forward for a major attack, heavy beams tipped with iron were lowered from the walls and crushed the engines. From the battlements, *ballistae* and stone-throwing catapults battered the Danes. The rocks smashed their shields and bashed out their brains, according to a chronicler of the conflict. The siege continued for almost a year. In that time, wagons loaded with burning turf were pushed against the city towers and blazing fire-ships tied against bridges. Several times the Danes fought off relieving armies, but all to no avail. Paris did not fall and eventually the Vikings accepted a tribute from the Frank king in return for their withdrawal.

The sophistication of Danish siege-machines may seem surprising but there is other evidence of such technology throughout this period. The continuity of Roman-style weaponry is revealed in an Anglo-Saxon riddle:

'I am the defender of my people.
Strengthened with wires and filled with gifts,
During the day I spit them forth.
The fuller I am the better I am.
I swallow dark weapons of war.
Bitter arrows and poisonous spears.
I have a good stomach.
Men seldom forget what passes through my mouth.'

Ballista is the answer. In another riddle —recorded in the 10th century, but probably far older — a battering-ram is described, 'A tree-trunk, once swathed in rich foliage, is now bound in chains and its head adorned with more sombre trappings.'

Several old English riddles are a highly imaginative interpretation of everyday objects and deal with many used in war. The harsh voice of the horn blown in battle : the shield weary of combat which can find no cure for its wounds from roots or herbs: a tree of four timbers, covered with silver and inlaid with jewels, with a goldhilted sword hanging from one of its branches. The last is a sword-rack. Many of the weapons used by both the Germans and the Scandinavians, though straight-forward in design, were skilfully adorned. Pattern-welded swords, still popular among the Vikings, were given dramatic names, according to their appearance and performance: such as 'Snake of wounds', 'Lightning flash of blood', and 'Mail-biter'. Viking swords usually had double-edged blades about 90 cm (3 ft) long. From the regularity of their mention in Scandinavian literature, it appears that Frankish swords from the Rhineland, as well as spear-blades, were strongly favoured. These imported, or stolen, blades were then given splendid hilts by native craftsmen. Straight cross-guards were made of bone, antler or ivory, which was then further encrusted with precious metals and stones according to the wealth of the warrior. Grips were

Finnish pattern-welded spearhead. The interlain iron and steel can be seen where the blade has been cleaned at the bottom. Now in the National Museum of Antiquities, Helsinki.

covered in leather while pommels were of metal, sometimes inscribed with the name of owner and maker. These swords were of such value that they could be passed on for generations.

An alternative, or addition to the sword, was the *scramasax*, a long single-edged knife. However, spears remained the commonest weapon, with lighter ones used for throwing and heavier ones for hand-to-hand. Spear-carrying and throwing horse-warriors continued to be an important element in battle and many Viking stirrups and spurs have been found. Aside from the spear, the battle-axe has emerged as the most characteristic weapon of the Northmen. Unlike the Frank throwing-axe, it was principally a broad-bladed close combat weapon that could be wielded with one hand or, with a longer shaft, become a terrifying two-handed weapon. Axe blades were also enriched and engraved. Shields, helmets and mail shirts followed much the same form as throughout the early medieval world. What certainly gave the Vikings in battle a material advantage over their adversaries was that as professional raiders they had greater access to a wide variety of ransacked weapons and armour and so, on the whole, were better equipped.

With secure bases in France and England, Vikings sailed further southwards, attacking Muslim Spain and bursting into the Mediterranean. They ransacked the city of Luna along the Italian coast, thinking it was Rome. There was little limit to the ambition of the Northmen. And yet, these achievements were largely accomplished by the Danes. The Norwegians were content to concentrate their attention on the north Atlantic and pursue daring exploration. The Swedes, on the other hand, made inroads into continental regimes like the Danes, but their chosen path was eastwards, along the rivers of Russia and eastern Europe, following perhaps the routes of earlier Germanic tribes, such as the Goths. For these warriors, the greatest pirate prizes were to be found along the coasts of the Black Sea. The Byzantines had little patience for these wild men from the North and called them plainly 'Barbarians'. Inevitably, Constantinople – still most splendid of all cities – came under siege several times from the Vikings. The city did not fall. On most occasions the Vikings were content with forcing the citizens to grant them lucrative trade concessions. Still, the Byzantines had a tough time of it and were so impressed with the Northmen as fighters that the emperors recruited them. They became the famed Varangian Guard, acting as personal bodyguards and an especially feared branch of the Byzantine army.

The daughter of one of the Eastern emperors, Anna Comnena, described the Northmen as 'Men who hung their swords and axes from their shoulders and regard their loyalty to the Emperor and his protection as a sacred duty, an inheritance to be handed from father to son.' The Greeks were impressed not only by their loyalty, but their physical size as well. They were nordic giants among Mediterranean men. The wealth to be obtained from serving the Byzantines was tremendous and whenever

Swedes returned to their homeland, the Scandinavians were deeply impressed by the travellers' rich clothes. One description of returning Varangian warriors pictures them in scarlet baggy trousers and riding on gilded saddles. Their leader wore a tunic and trousers of silk, over which hung a cloak of scarlet. His sword hilt was ornamented with gold thread wound round the grip. On his head he wore a gilded helmet and carried a scarlet shield. Wherever they stopped, native nordic women could not keep their eyes off the brilliant warriors. Another description of the eastern Vikings again mentions their baggy trousers, fastened around the knee, but adds kaftans and tall hats. The Varangian Guard was established around the end of the 10th century: for a century before this, the Northmen had been untamed marauders.

With the subjugation of various Slavonic, Finnish and Eurasian tribes, the Swedish Vikings of the 9th century became the rulers of western Russia, where they were known as the Rus. From their southern capital at Kiev, and from surrounding strongholds, several ambitious campaigns were carried out, ranging from the Caspian to the Black Sea. Not least of these were their attacks on Constantinople. Around the year 907, King Oleg of Kiev led a fleet of upwards of 200 ships against the Byzantines. Each ship carried forty men. Large as this may seem, far greater Viking forces were also recorded.

Compared to his own ships, Emperor Leo VI noted that the boats the Rus used were 'smaller, lighter, faster crafts, because sailing into the Black Sea through the rivers, they cannot use bigger ships.' Sometimes the Rus attacked overland. *The Russian Primary Chronicle,* compiled by Nestor in the 12th century, states that Oleg's assault on Constantinople was by ship and by horse. The employment of mounted warriors does suggest that this was a major campaign, although the chronicle may well be at fault. In the main, most Viking raids were from the sea. To counter these, the Byzantines drew a massive chain across the inlet of the Golden Horn to the north of their capital, but faced with such an obstacle, the Rus merely beached their boats and ravaged the surrounding communities on foot. Frequently these conflicts were settled with tributes and a trade treaty. To Oleg, the Byzantines gave brocade sails for his Viking ships and silk sails for the Slavs that fought with him. These fancy sails were soon torn by the wind and they reverted to ones of canvas.

When the Byzantines did fight back against the Rus raiders, one of their most effective weapons was Greek Fire. The pirate fleet of King Igor suffered badly from this in 941. Surrounding a smaller Byzantine force and expecting easy plunder, the Vikings were suddenly enveloped in a blazing mixture of crude oil and other combustibles pumped through metal tubes mounted on their victims' ships. With their clothes and hair aflame, Rus sailors flung themselves into the sea rather than endure the sulphurous, burning hell on board. The Viking fleet was annihilated. The terror provoked by these early flame-throwers encouraged the Rus to return home with tales maintaining that the Byzantines possessed the very lightning from heaven. Byzantine craftsmen capitalised on this awe and designed metal tubes in the shape of weird animals, so that the fire spewed from their mouths. It is little wonder that stories of fire-breathing dragons were frequent among the Northmen. It may also be that mythological accounts from Scandinavia of special tunics which made the wearer invulnerable, actually derived from the flame-proof clothes, woven from asbestos and silk, that the Byzantines are said to have devised. Interestingly, one northern saga has an alternative description of just such a protective garment. To defend himself against a fire-breathing dragon, the warrior hero dipped a coarse woollen coat in tar until it was matted and then rolled it in sand to give it an impregnable surface.

The chief fear-inducing weapon the Vikings possessed was themselves. The impression that their nordic stature and ferocity made on the Byzantines has already been mentioned but there were, however, a special group of warriors amongst the Vikings, in both the east and the west, who made even their own comrades feel uneasy. They were the hard-men in whom courage was mingled with madness. They were the *berserkr*. Wearing no armour, but clad in bear-fur and other animal skins, these terrifying

Danish decorated sword hilt from Hedeby, one of the largest Viking settlements. Now in the Schleswig-Holstein Landesmuseum.

warriors rushed into battle mowing down everyone before them. They had no fear, for their rage of bloodlust overcame the pain of their wounds. Howling like wolves, they bit their shields, and when their weapons were shattered through frenzied blows, they tore their enemies apart with bare hands in a fury of animal strength. This crazed state has been ascribed to the taking of hallucinogenics, but it seems more likely that it was simply the alcohol-enhanced action of wild men. Hardened psychopaths have accompanied every army and robber band throughout history, and it was probably the perverse thrill they obtained from violence that fuelled these warriors onto superhuman feats. Such human beasts have always been men to avoid and it is not surprising that the Vikings themselves considered these warriors to be possessed – turning into werewolves under cover of night. For most of the time, they managed to hide their dark nature, but once they got whiff of a fight, their calm character was unbalanced and these warriors became ravening animals again.

Though renowned for their ferocity, the majority of Vikings were, in reality, no more ferocious than other Barbarian warriors. The Vikings did, however, possess one unique attribute which gave them a very definite edge over many of their contemporaries. The Scandinavian mastery of water-borne warfare can be compared with the excellent horsemanship of the steppe warriors. It has been said that the seamanship of the Vikings has been overestimated: after all, the majority of their raids either closely followed the continental coasts or simply penetrated European waterways. This might have been true of the Danes and the Swedes, but the navigational feats of the Norwegians were quite remarkable. This aside, the quality of the Vikings as ocean-going warriors is hardly the point. Very few battles were actually fought at sea. One account of just such an armed encounter, around AD 1000, shows that the ensuing battle was more like an action fought on land than a battle requiring naval skills.

When Olaf Tryggvason of Norway sailed out against an alliance of Scandinavian rulers, he roped his ships together so that they were not so much a fleet as a floating platform. Fortunately for Olaf, when the two sides clashed, he had the advantage of craft with higher decks. Anchors and boathooks were hurled at the opposing ships to secure them so that warriors could charge onto each others' decks. The main missile weapons in action were the usual bows and light throwing spears employed on land. At times, stones were also used, either thrown or powered by slings. There was no attempt by either side to ram or outmanoeuvre each other. As fortunes changed, the Scandinavian alliance forced the Norwegian crews on the outermost boats to retreat inwards. Winning ship after ship, the Scandinavians slashed the ropes keeping together the ships and so increasingly isolated their opponents on the splendid carved and gilded Long Serpent ship of Olaf. A fierce last stand took place, during which many of Olaf's warriors threw themselves into the sea rather than be captured. At the end, after throwing spears with both hands and wielding his sword until it was

Vikings attack an Arab encampment. Both the Danes and the Swedes clashed with the Muslims, but they never seriously challenged their dominion of the Mediterranean. From Guizot's *L'Histoire de France*, 1870.

blunt, Olaf joined his faithful warriors and plunged to his death amongst the waves. Even such a major marine combat as this was probably not fought on the open-sea but in a bay or river mouth. It is little wonder that after their initial foray into the Mediterranean, the Danes did not try to challenge the naval might of the Arabs: or that when the Swedes decided to attack Constantinople, they waited until the Byzantine fleet was away on other business.

The strength of the Vikings lay in the amphibious nature of their raids. No other group of warriors could equal this versatility. In the West, once the Danes had sailed their ships up onto a beach, they could then take themselves deep inland on horse-back. Alternatively, once the great rivers of France proved too shallow ever for their slender craft, they took to smaller canoes and penetrated even further, finally advancing on foot to subdue a city. In the East, the Swedes were masters of the waterways of Eurasia. From their island or riverbank fortresses, they launched raiding campaigns numbering hundreds of boats against powerful bastions. If needs be, as in their assault on Costantinople in 907, they mounted their ships on rollers and let the wind fill their sails to help them overland. All this gave the Vikings the primary military advantages of speed, mobility and surprise.

Travelling deep into unknown territory, the Vikings fought a battle against the harsh environment as violent and taxing as any test of arms. The hardship and fears of this roving life are best conveyed in an Anglo-Saxon poem commonly called *The Seafarer*. Probably based on the accounts of the same warrior exile described in *The Wanderer*, it opens with the wild weather conditions endured on the North Sea. The Seafarer takes his turn at night-watch. The ship dips and rises perilously near a rocky coast-line. His feet are frozen to the deck. Icicles hang all around him. Hail stones beat down. His only comfort is the cry of the sea-birds. But these serve only to remind him of the laughter of the drinking-hall.

'How can the land dweller, living in a city and flushed with wine, know the suffering of sailing?' asks the seafarer, 'And yet, despite snow from the north, frost and hail, deep down there is a yearning to undertake a journey. To see a new land, a foreign people. But there is no man, so brave or so bold, that he does not feel fear when venturing on the sea. All thought of the joy of music, the receiving of rings, ecstasy in a woman, all worldly pleasures, are replaced by the relentless rolling of the waves. But even then, the mind travels over the sea, across the whale's domain, to strange new regions and the spirit is urged onwards. This life is fleeting and the best a warrior can hope for is to win the respect of those living after him. The finest monument is to achieve noble and daring deeds in this world so his name may be honoured by his children.'

In these lines, the wanderlust of the warrior overcoming the dread and danger of roaming in an alien, hostile world, is potently expressed. It is an impressive evocation of the essential character of the Germanic Barbarian.

The relentless plainsmen

THE AVARS,
MAGYARS
AND
MONGOLS:
THE
6th TO 13th
CENTURIES

The Huns forever lurked in the minds of medieval men. They were the most notorious of the warriors from the eastern plains: all others followed in their wake. Four centuries after their destruction, Notker, chronicler of Charlemagne, recalled a tale told to him when a boy by a veteran soldier. 'The land of the Huns used to be encircled by nine rings,' said the old man. 'These rings were fortifications. Very wide. Many miles separated them. The defences of each ring were built of logs of oak, beech and fir. These constructions were then filled with stones and heavy clay. They were eight paces deep and eight paces high. On top of the ramparts, sods of earth were piled. Small trees were then planted along each ring so that when cut back and trained to bend forward, they presented an impenetrable screen of sharp branches and dense foliage. On the land between each ring, farms and houses were laid out, but so placed that any news of invasion could be transmitted by the blowing of a horn.'

Such a system of earthworks was not beyond the capabilities of early medieval rulers, as the Danework of King Godfred demonstrated, but no evidence of these particular ramparts has been found, and this story is essentially an indication of the fantastic achievements attributed to the Huns. It is significant of the impact of the Huns that for hundreds of years afterwards, eastern mounted raiders from the steppes were still called by that name. For the warriors that Notker and his story teller called Huns were, in actual fact, another Eurasian confederation – the Avars.

The Avars were no new menace. They had ravaged the Empire of the Franks over two centuries before and fabulous reports of their origin had been heard in Constantinople. A pack of griffins, half eagle, half lion, had erupted in the wastes of Asia and before them they drove a ferocious group of warriors. No sooner had the Eastern emperors seen the last of the Huns than this next onslaught of horse-archers was upon them, perhaps driven on by droughts or the expanding campaigns of an even fiercer people. The Avars were essentially of Turkish origin, from around the Caucasus and southern Russia. Among their ranks were the descendants of the hordes of Attila who had retreated to the lands north of the Black Sea. As they pushed westwards, the Bulgars and Slavs were disturbed into action. 'These Barbarians have reduced the whole of the Balkans to a second Scythian desert,' concluded Procopius in his *Secret History* of the reign of Justinian. The region was scarred by war, disease and famine. Any major armed resistance to the raiders was quashed by the Emperor who wished to employ the various Barbarian factions against each other.

With their marauding unopposed, the Avars, Slavs and Bulgars became even more daring and outrageous. So that in the end, shocked by the sight of their ransacked farms, and with their wives and children enslaved, Balkan civilians and farmers formed themselves into groups of local resistance. Often they were successful, ambushing bandits laden with booty, but once word of this reached the Imperial authorities, government troops were sent to harass the farmers, forcing them to return the horses and plunder they had taken from the raiders. To the inhabitants of the Balkans, the Byzantines were as great a menace as the Barbarians. Within the massive walls of Constantinople, the close presence of the Eurasian nomads served only to inspire a new fashion among the wild young men of the city. To set themselves apart, one street gang – the Blues – wore bizarre clothing after the style of the 'Huns', that is, the Avars. They cut the hair on the front of their heads right back, but allowed the hair behind to hang down in a tangled mass. They wore tunics belted very tight at the waist that then spread out to their shoulders, giving them the appearance of muscle men. In addition, they wore the capes, trousers and shoes typical of steppe warriors. This gang caused much trouble in the city: robbing people at night, rioting during the day. Little was done to stop them, for the Emperor was said to favour them over the Greens, another gang deriving from opposing sports supporters.

In their wars against the Byzantines, the Avars employed guile as much as brute force. During the reign of Tiberius II, towards the end of the 6th century, the Kagan of the Avars asked the Emperor if he would be gracious enough to let him share some of the luxuries of civilisation by having Byzantine technicians build a bath house for him. No doubt seeing this as a sign of future good relations, the Emperor despatched expert craftsmen immediately. But when they arrived, it was not a complex of saunas and hot and cold pools that the Kagan was expecting them to build. He wanted a bridge across the Danube. At sword-point the Byzantines acquiesced, and the Avars surged over the river into the Balkans. On another occasion, Avar attempts to outwit the Byzantines backfired. In 562, merchant envoys were instructed to travel to Constantinople on behalf of the Avars and there acquire arms and armour skilfully manufactured by the Byzantines, thus equipping the Avars for a campaign against the self-same citizens. But Imperial intelligence was one step ahead. Once the merchants had handed over their money and bundled up the weaponry, they were seized by the Byzantine authorities and their goods confiscated. In this way, the Avars made an unwitting contribution to their enemy's balance of trade.

Pair of 9th century bronze-gilt spurs, either Avar or Slav. The prick points are decorated with helmeted heads. From Mikulcice in Czechoslovakia, courtesy of the Archaeological Institute of the Slovakian Academy of Sciences, Nitra.

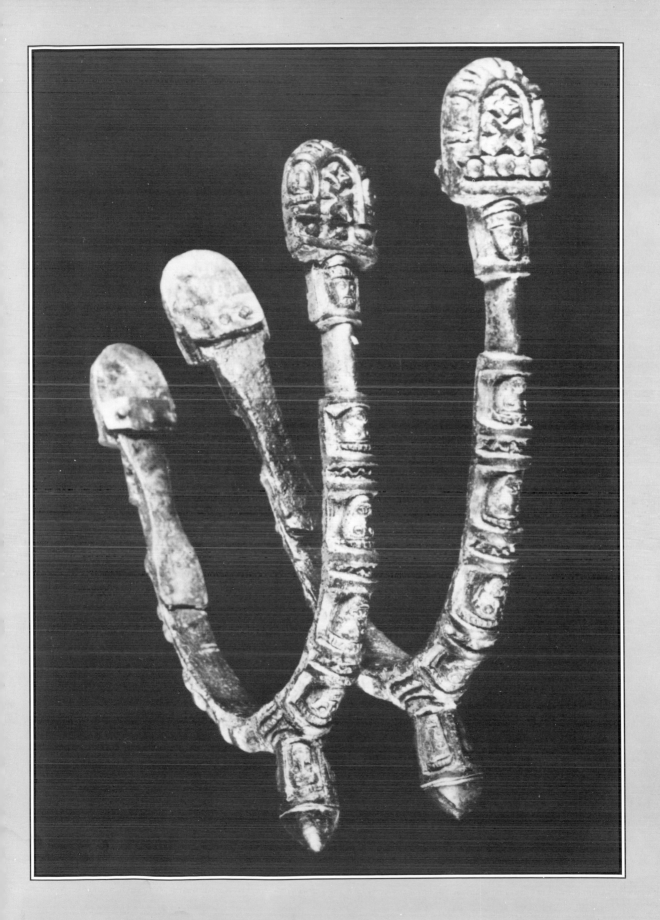

By the 8th century, the Avars had left the wealth of the Byzantines to other raiders and were in conflict with the Germanic kingdoms of the West. Settled in the old Roman province of Pannonia, the dwellings of their Khan grew splendid with all their pickings from Italy, France and Germany. The Avar raiders were naturally excellent horsemen. The use of stirrups was widespread among them, and highly ornate spurs have been found where the prick-points feature little helmeted faces. In addition to their composite bows, spears and pattern-welded swords, it appears from archaeological evidence that they may also have favoured battle-axes, perhaps adopted from the Slavic tribesmen who had followed the Germanic migrations but were now dominated by the Avars. The Franks, like all Germanic warriors, were never really happy fighting highly mobile horse-archers. With their feigned retreats and reluctance to close-in until they had emptied their quivers, the keeness of the Franks for combat with sword and spear was constantly frustrated. And yet, over the course of a decade, Charlemagne and his retainers brought the Avar menace to heel. Warfare is obviously not just a matter of the most effective fighting fashion winning through. Political and strategic factors all contribute to victory or defeat, and it seems that Charlemagne may well have caught the Avars at a time when their control of Avar terriory was weakening, while his political control was patently overwhelming. There is, however, a distinct difference in the manner of Frankish warfare under Charlemagne, which appears unique to his period.

As stated previously, the bow was not a weapon widely used by Germanic horse-warriors, for despite its obvious effectiveness, it was not considered noble enough to displace the sword and spear of the mounted man. Nevertheless, in a letter to the Abbot Fulrad, Charlemagne instructed him to supply his army with horsemen equipped specifically with shield, lance, sword, dagger, and bow and arrows. Elsewhere, in a manuscript of 803, each landlord is asked to equip their warriors with a lance, shield, a bow and two bowstrings plus 12 arrows. In this *Capitulare Aquisgranense*, there is a sentence that says that two men are required to have these weapons between them. This may suggest that a mounted warrior was expected to carry lance and sword, while a dismounted man — a squire, perhaps — used the bow. This would certainly fit the status of weapons common in Western Europe. However, the summons to Abbot Fulrad does not make this distinction and some military historians have suggested that Charlemagne armed his horse-warriors with bows especially to counter the Avars, although the skill of these Frankish archers cannot have been as refined as that of the Eurasians.

That Carolingian horse-warriors did not wholly adapt themselves to the ways of the Avars is perhaps indicated by their slow adoption of the stirrup, an oriental device. The earliest illustrations of warriors using stirrups in Western Europe come from Carolingian manuscripts illuminated in the latter half of the 9th century. Consistently in these pictures, some

Model of a horse showing an 8th century central Asian saddle. From Astana Cemetery. Now in the British Museum, London.

122

FIGURE OF A HORSE
ASTĀNA CEMETERY
c. 640 — 750 A.D.
"Innermost Asia" Ast. III. 3. 037. Plate XCVIII.

123

riders are shown using them and some are not. Just as amongst the Arabs over a century before, some conservative warriors probably considered the use of the stirrup a sign of weakness. Certainly, it seems that the introduction of the stirrup to Western warfare did not have as major an impact as some historians have ascribed to it. It was adopted slowly and its main influence on later mounted warriors appears to have been to encourage a stiff-legged riding posture rather than one in which legs are bent so as to clutch the horse. This meant warriors could stand in the saddle, but the introduction of the stirrup did not increase significantly the number of horse-borne warriors. Riding was largely a matter of status and wealth. Nor did it further the use of the lance among mounted men. The image of a warrior now enabled to crash into an adversary with his lance without falling off because of his stirrups is a false one. Firstly, a horse will rarely charge into a static obstacle, like a wall of shield-bearing men. Secondly, lances had in any case been used effectively before the stirrup, and were best employed in single-combat against another horseman or when pursuing a broken formation of fleeing foot-soldiers.

Despite uncertainty regarding the Frankish use of both the bow and the stirrup, the Carolingian war-machine was undoubtedly well organised. In the written instructions issued from Charlemagne's various royal residences, there are fascinating descriptions of the wagon-trains that would be used to carry the burden of his campaigns against the pagans. 'The wagons that accompany our warriors as war carts shall be well-constructed,' says one manuscript. 'Their coverings shall be made of animal skins and sewn together so that when crossing a river, the provisions inside will remain dry. It is also our wish that a goodly amount of flour and wine shall be placed in each cart.' Another manuscript lists further the equipment to be carried in each wagon, 'Food in abundance, stone handmills, adzes, axes, carpenters' tools, and slings with men who can use them properly. Stones are to brought for these slings, on 20 pack-horses if needs be . . .' These latter weapons translated as slings may well be catapults or *ballistae*. With such logistical back-up, in the Roman manner, Charlemagne undoubtedly had an advantage over his less organised adversaries. This is probably what brought him victory against the Avars. That the Franks may also have possessed more sophisticated weapons and armour than their enemies is suggested by the repeated prohibition on arms trading with foreign countries. 'Concerning traders who travel in the territories of the Slavs and the Avars,' begins a *Capitulary* of 805. 'They must not take weapons and coats of mail with them to sell. If they are caught carrying them, their entire stock is to be confiscated.'

The Franks were not the only Imperialists worried about giving away their military advantages. The Greek Fire of the Byzantines was an obsessively guarded secret weapon. Emperor Constantine VII in writing to his son in the 10th century continued the tradition of secrecy. 'If you are ever asked to divulge information about the making of liquid fire discharged through tubes, you must reply, "This was revealed by God through an angel to the great and holy Constantine, the first Christian Emperor. And we are assured by the faithful witness of our fathers and grandfathers that it should only be manufactured among the Christians and in their capital city and nowhere else." For it happened once that one of our military commanders was bribed by the heathens and handed over some fire to them. God could not leave such a transgression unavenged and so when the man entered the holy church of God, a fire-ball was sent down from heaven and completely consumed him.'

From the 7th to the 9th century, the Avars dominated central Europe. Over the same period, to the east, the Bulgars controlled those parts of the Balkans they had wrestled from the Byzantines as well as the lower Danube area. To the east of them, in southern Russia, there was the mighty kingdom of the Khazars. Like the Avars, both these latter tribal confederations were essentially Turkish. Amongst them were the remnants of the Huns. In their midst, also, were Slavic tribes who, though largely subjugated, increasingly rose in revolt against their Eurasian masters. The Avars shamelessly exploited the Slaves who lived under their authority. They spent the winter with these Slavs, sleeping with their wives and daughters and living off Slav tributes. In battle, the Avars were said to herd the Slavs into their front lines, waiting for them to blunt the fighting and only then joining in the battle to insure victory and a majority of the plunder. Eventually, the half-caste sons of the Avars and their Slav women found the situation intolerable and rose successfully against the nomad bandits. Like Notker after him, the chronicler of these acts, Fredegar, also called the Avars 'Huns'.

The Bulgars and Khazars were mail-clad horse-warriors with bow, sword and spear. Frequently fighting among each other, they also clashed with the Byzantines, the Arabs, the Slavs and the Rus. The Khazars were the most powerful of the steppe confederations. Their tribes controlled land north of the Caucasian mountains, from the Black Sea to the Caspian. Because of this position, they proved a useful bulwark against any Muslim invasion of eastern Europe via the Caucasus. The Byzantines frequently entered into peace treaties with them. Because of the profit, both political and material, to be obtained from this role as neutral third power, the Khazar leaders had to think carefully about their religious status. By remaining nomadic heathens, they would gain neither the respect of the Arabs nor the Byzantines, being regarded merely as useful Barbarians. However, if they chose either Christianity or Islam, that would mean spiritual, and thus political, alignment with either Caliph or Emperor. In the event, the Khazars shrewdly chose to convert to that other faith of the People of the Book – Judaism. Subsequently, a union of nomadic Aryan Jews dominated southern Russia for several hundred years. An Arabic chronicler described some of their traits.

'When the Khazars bring back their plunder from a raid, they pool it together in the camp. The leader then takes for himself what he wishes and leaves the rest to be divided amongst his warriors. When embarking for a campaign, the Khazar leader instructs every man to carry with him a sharp stake. On halting for the night, these stakes are then placed around the camp with shields hanging from them so as to form a palisade.'

In a passage more difficult to interpret, the Arabic sources conjure up a picture of the Khazar warlord riding before his army surrounded by a vanguard carrying either lighted candles and torches or bright, reflective metal discs. Such weird illumination probably acted as a kind of signalling or as a badge of rank. It may also have had a religious signifiance.

The domination of Eurasia by the Avars, Bulgars and the Khazars came to an end at the close of the 9th century. Migrating southwards from the Ural mountains, a group of tribes closely related to the Finns entered upon the battle-ground of the steppes. These were the Magyars. At first, they were subject to the Khazars, collecting taxes for their overlords from the Slavs. During this period the Magyars mixed with the Turkish tribesmen, and would have become proficient horsemen and archers, if they had not already been. Certainly, by the last decades of the 9th century, when intertribal warfare intensified, the Magyars met their rivals on equal terms. In this ferocious activity, north of the Black Sea, a Turkish tribe – the Pechenegs – loomed large. The Byzantine Emperor Constantine VII recorded that, 'their neighbours always look on the Pechenegs with dread and are held in check by them.' Even the Rus could not carry out raids into the

MALE FIGURE,
MINGOI. c. 8TH - 10TH CENT.
"Serindia". Plate CXXXIII. Mi. xi. 0064.

Black Sea unless they were at peace with these nomads. For whenever the Viking raiders reached cataracts along the southern Russian waterways, they were forced to shoulder their boats overland to quieter waters: and once caught on the riverbank by a band of hostile Pechenegs, the Rus were easily overwhelmed and cut to pieces.

The Pechenegs were described as having 'weapons in plenty, belts of silver, standards and short spears, and decorated trumpets which they sound in battle.' It was these warriors who, according to the Emperor Constantine, were responsible for shifting the Magyars into Europe. While the Magyars were away from their families, raiding the territories of the Bulgars, the Pechenegs, encouraged by the Bulgar ruler, tore into the land of the Magyars and devastated their homes, slaughtering their wives, children and the few guards left behind. With their Khazar allies in decline, and faced with the incursions of the Pechenegs and the Rus, the Magyars may well have seen their move westwards as the easiest option. Entering eastern Europe, they clashed unsuccessfully with the Bulgars. Having better luck against the Avars, already crushed and fragmented by Charlemagne, the Magyars pitched their tents in central Europe. From the plains of Hungary, the Magyars carried out relentless raids against the Germanic kingdoms of the West. A terror which lasted for over half a century.

'Pavia is burning.
Winds increase the fire.
Magyar mobs set upon citizens
choking, fleeing from the flames.
Pavia is burning.
Down the streets the blaze spreads.
Women and children are trampled down,
a holy priest is slain.
Pavia is burning.
Gold melts through chests
hidden deep in sewers.
Streams of silver hiss
and bubble in the gutter.
Pavia is burning.'

In these lines from a poem by Liutprand, Bishop of Cremona, a devastation to equal that of Attila's sack of Aquileia is described. It comes from Liutprands's *Antapodosis*, a revealing account of Magyar incursions in the first quarter of the 10th century. His story begins with Arnulf, King of the eastern Carolingian territories, letting the Magyars into Western Europe. Hoping that the nomads would distract and hinder his enemies, Arnulf broke down the great earthworks that prevented the Magyars from advancing any further. Once in, the Magyars embarked on an orgy of pillage against Arnulf's enemies: but as soon as Arnulf was dead, even his own people were not safe from Magyar raids.

'No man ever wished more desperately for food or water than these savages desire a fight,' exclaimed Liutprand, 'their only joy is in battle.' Quoting an ancient historian, Jordanes, he then ascribed to the Magyars an old Hun custom. 'They scar their babies with knives so that they might bear the pain of wounds before receiving milk from their mothers' breasts.' Again, the latest Eurasian invaders and the Huns were seen as one and the same. Fast losing hold of his recently acquired kingdom, Louis, son of Arnulf, gathered his forces together and confronted the raiders on the plains near the city of Augsburg. It was barely daybreak when the Magyars rode on the Bavarians in their camp. Yawning and rousing themselves for the day's confrontation, German warriors were suddenly assaulted from all sides by a hail of arrows. Some never awoke – transfixed in their beds. Darting to and fro, the Magyars caused great havoc. Stumbling out of their tents, with mail only half on, warriors had their heads split by Magyar sabres. Rallying themselves amidst the panic, Louis' men dashed after a retreating band of horse-archers but, of course, in familiar fashion, this was a deception and the ambush was drawn tight. Magyars pounced on the Germans and Louis was beaten, narrowly escaping the slaughter himself. After such a defeat, Bavaria, Swabia, Saxony and eastern France lay open. Villages and monasteries were sacked and burnt, while clerics wondered what on earth their lords were doing about the Church's defence. More concerned about pursuing their dynastic feuds, however, the majority of German warlords tamely paid the Hungarians a tribute. Sitting out the storm behind the walls of their castles, the barons and dukes used this emergency as an excuse to tax their own people – part of which they kept themselves.

Italy had always proved attractive to Barbarians and was no less so to the Magyars. On their first journey south of the Alps, their scouts reported that though they were unsure of the strength of the Italians as fighters, they saw that their numbers were great and their towns well fortified. The Magyars rode back to their homeland and spent the winter in preparation for a more substantial campaign. According to Liutprand, they spent these months making armour, sharpening their weapons and training their young men with military exercises. The next spring they returned to Italy, passing through the regions of Aquileia, Verona and Pavia. Berengar, Carolingian king of northern Italy, had never even heard of the Magyars. Nevertheless, he quickly raised a force from his subjects that outnumbered the invaders three to one. Confronted by such an army, the Hungarians chose flight rather than fight, and swam across the river Adda before the might of the Italian warriors. Many Magyars were drowned in the panic and those who clambered up onto the other bank offered to return all their booty to the Christians. The Italians felt insulted and rejected this sign of weakness.

The Magyars further retreated to the plains around Verona. There, an Italian vanguard caught up with them. In the skirmish, the cocksure Italians were thrashed. But mindful of the rest of the army, the Hungarians again trekked homeward. Finally, their horses exhausted, the Magyars were forced to make camp beyond the river Brenta. The Italians jeered at them from the other side of the water. Once more, the Magyars offered to surrender their captured goods, their prisoners, arms and horses. They swore never to invade Italy and offered their sons as hostages. Sensing an easy and prestigious victory, the Italians said no, 'We do not accept pleas of surrender from dogs that have already given themselves up.' Driven to despair, and seeing no better way out, the Hungarians readied themselves for combat: they had nothing to lose for 'to fall fighting like men is not to die, but to live.' As was their manner, the Magyars took the offensive. Crossing the river surreptitiously, they surprised the Italians while the latter were resting and eating. Dismounted and scattered among their tents, they were easy prey for the Magyars. Some Italians, though equipped and ready, held back from the fray, seeing that the Magyars were conveniently annihilating their rivals. The Hungarians gave no quarter.

On the death of King Conrad (Louis' successor) the Magyars again decided on a show of strength. The election of a German king was a crucial time for the Hungarians as a new monarch frequently chose to begin his reign by refusing to continue any regular tribute. They therefore advanced into the territory of the Saxon king Henry, the new overlord of the Germans. Henry was ill at the time, but regardless of this he gathered a strong force about him: all men above the age of 13 were required to render him military service. Meanwhile, the Magyars had crossed the Saxon border enslaving women and children, and massacring all men as a warning of their ruthlesness. Magyar scouts came across the Saxon army assembled at Merseburg and at once rode back to their masters. Henry decided to deliver the message personally and his army moved swiftly upon the raiders.

Before the two forces clashed, the *Kyrie eleison* of the Christian Germans rang out, 'Lord have mercy upon us'. The heathens countered with an awesome battle-chant. By now used to the damaging tactics of the Hungarian horse-archers, King Henry ordered his horse-warriors to advance together, and not let those with faster mounts dash ahead and be swallowed up by the Magyar horde. As they thundered forward the Magyars let fly with their arrows. Expecting this, the Saxons raised their shields and caught the first volley upon them. Spurring their horses onwards, the Germans endeavoured to reach the Magyars before they could unleash another deadly cloud. Such tactics sound more impressive than they really were for surely the raising of a shield to protect oneself from arrows was common-sense. Perhaps it was the sense of order that was new. With the heavily-clad Saxons crashing towards them, the Magyars suddenly lost their courage and broke before the onslaught. The Hungarian raiders had been checked. This battle and the previous defeat of King Louis were placed by Liutprand at the beginning of both kings' reigns, giving

Central Asian warrior in scale armour or mail. The armour of the Avars, Bulgars and Khazars was influenced by their powerful eastern neighbours, and many probably looked like this. From Mingoi, now in the British Museum, London.

130

the Magyars a good excuse for their raids. Later historians, however, have generally placed these battles around 910 and 933 respectively.

With the German states proving too hot for comfort, the Magyars turned southwards again. In 924, a large Hungarian force invaded Italy and amidst the carnage, Pavia was burnt to the ground; Liutprand's town of birth. Times had changed, however, and western warlords were no longer willing meekly to pay tribute. Otto, another vigorous Saxon king, caught some Magyar raiders in a marsh along the Lower Elbe and savaged them. Never again would Saxony hear the hoof-beats of the Hungarians. Later, the Bavarians followed this up by smashing the raiders on their frontier and then plunging into Magyar territory. Hungarian encampments were ransacked. This time it was Magyar women and children who became part of the intensive slave trade practised by both heathen and Christian warlords. Determined to end their bad luck, the Magyars broke in upon a civil war between German princes in 954 and rode through Bavaria and into France in a major show of strength. Predictably, as the Magyars passed through, various feuding German factions could not resist trying to employ them on their side, but this time the nomads would not be diverted from their task. Unintentionally, this invasion strengthened the hand of Otto for he now marched into Bavaria at the head of a liberating army, determined to forget party politics and confront the common foe. Missing each other, the Magyars returned to their homeland determined to repeat the action.

The Hungarian horde that entered Bavaria in 955 was the biggest that central Europe had seen for many years. It seemed as if the Magyars wanted to settle once and for all their right to range unrestricted across Europe. That summer they swarmed around the city of Augsburg, the site of a previous victory. After denuding the surrounding districts, they approached the walls of the city with siege-engines; once again demonstrating that steppe warriors were no less sophisticated militarily than their town-dwelling opponents. With earthworks dug, tents pitched, the massive machines were pushed forward by Slav slaves whipped from behind. Suddenly the siege came to a halt. News had reached the Magyars that an army led by Otto was fast approaching. They readied themselves for battle. With Saxons, Bavarians, Franconians, Swabians and Bohemians riding beneath his banners, Otto made camp near the river Lech, a tributary of the Danube. Bolstered by warriors slipping out of Augsburg and numerous Slav auxiliaries, the German forces probably numbered about 5,000. Calling together their raiding parties with the aid of smoke signals, the Magyars were commonly believed to outnumber the Germans. That night, a fast was ordered among the Christians to prepare them spiritually for the coming combat: many warriors were probably too tense to eat anyway.

On the morning of battle, the German warlords swore allegiance to each other. Many a conflict in the past had been lost through rivals holding back in the expectation of their competitors being wiped out by the enemy. The Christian host then said mass and advanced with

lances and standards held high. They rode forward in eight groups, according to nationality. Otto's Saxons moved beneath the banner of Saint Michael, the heavenly vanquisher of the Devil. With the Lech to the left of them, its banks overgrown with foliage, the Germans did not notice a contingent of Magyars moving rapidly along their flank on the other side of the river. These Magyars then crossed the river and set upon the end group of Germans guarding the army's baggage train. With arrows hissing about them and the Hungarians howling like wolves, the Bohemian and Swabian rearguard faltered and fled. Disaster seemed to have struck Otto at once. With fighting already encountered in front and now a third of his army routed in the rear, encirclement appeared imminent.

Desperately, Otto despatched Duke Conrad to deal with the crisis behind him. Conrad was a bold and well respected leader and his presence rallied the remaining Franconians. They counter-attacked and freed many prisoners from the Magyars who had become diverted from battle by the task of

Magyar raiders set fire to a German homestead from a late 19th century illustration. In the 10th century the Magyars revived Western fears about horse-archers from the eastern plains.

132

French photograph of a Mongol warrior taken at the turn of this century. His sprouting quiver and bowcase with its composite bow – which is almost as tall as him – have always been characteristic of all Eurasian steppe warriors.

carrying away their booty. The crux of the battle now switched to the front. Here, according to a speech put into the mouth of Otto by the chronicler Widukind, the Saxon King encouraged his men with the fact that the Magyars were not as well equipped. 'They surpass us, I know, in numbers,' gasped Otto, 'but neither in weapons nor in courage. We know also that they are quite without the help of God, which is of the greatest comfort to us.' It is unlikely that anyone could have heard such a brave speech amidst the clamour and clang of fighting. But was it true? Certainly, leading German warriors would have been wrapped in a splendour of mail, with heavy shields, helmets, lances and swords. While, as steppe warriors, the Magyars may well have been more lightly armoured: depending more on the efficiency of their bows. However, most warriors at this time in both Europe and Asia wore mail, while as professional plunderers the Magyars would have been armed with the very best weapons and armour. Indeed, much of their armoury would have been the same as that of the Germans, for it was from them that the Magyars had stolen it. But whatever the relative strength in arms, the advantage in spirit and morale seems to have shifted to the Germans, who charged the Magyars successfully.

In the hard slog of hand to hand, the bravest warriors of both sides clashed fiercely while others turned and ran. It was a hot summer day and in the heat of combat, Conrad, hero of the battle, loosened the mail around his helmet. At once, an Hungarian arrow flashed through the air and struck him in the throat. He choked and fell from his horse. But now, even the strongest of the Magyar warriors were overwhelmed by the triumphant Germans, and they joined the general rout. Leaping into the river Lech, some drowned when the bank on the opposite side collapsed under their weight. Others hid in outlying villages, but were surrounded and cremated within the huts. High with victory, the Germans pursued the fleeing Magyars over the next two days. Hungarian noblemen laden with gold necklaces and silver cruciform bosses on their shields were captured and hanged like common criminals. It was this ruthless follow up to the victory on the Lechfeld that was decisive in breaking the back of the Magyars. Unfortunately for the natives of Augsburg, it was also this orgy of man-hunting that achieved a local destruction as bad as any inflicted by the Hungarians. Nevertheless, the action did bring an end to the Magyar raids.

Leaderless and with so many warriors lying dead and mutilated on the trails of Bavaria back to the eastern plains, the Magyars never again invaded German territories. The Magyars had lost their fury. Over future generations, Hungary became a settled European kingdom where Bavarian missionaries carried out a successful job of conversion. By the end of the 10th century, it was the Hungarians who were sending tributes to the Germans. The prestige of Otto and his dynasty rose considerably as a result of this victory. Acknowledging the end of a great Eurasian menace, the Byzantines sent him presents of congratulation and called him 'emperor'. From the jealous guardians. of the Eastern Roman Empire, this was high praise indeed.

With the Magyars tamed, the West remained free of steppe warriors for three hundred years. Raiding was always a problem, but this existed as much among feudal lords as more nomadic people, and on the whole no major tribal confederation from the east threatened the stability of central and western Europe. Then, in 1238 in Yarmouth, England, the price of herrings plummeted. Fifty fish could be had for just one piece of silver. That year, German merchants from across the North Sea had stayed away. They stayed away because the people of north Germany were in fear of invasion by 'a monstrous and inhuman race of men'. Matthew Paris, English chronicler, recorded the fantastic reports that reached him from the continent of this new menace.

'The men are of the nature of beasts. They thirst after and drink blood. They clothe themselves in the skins of bulls and are armed with iron lances. They are short in stature and thick-set, compact in their bodies. Their horses are very swift and able to perform a journey of three days in one.

They have swords and daggers with one edge – sabres – and are excellent archers. They take their herds with them, as also their wives, who are brought up to war the same as men. Their chief is a ferocious man named Khan. The people are very numerous. The come with the force of lightning into the territories of the Christians and are believed to have been sent as a plague on mankind.' In this passage are echoes of earlier descriptions of Huns, Avars and Magyars. But this time, the oriental nomads were called Tartars, after Tartarus, a mythical place of punishment in the classical underworld. They are known today as the Mongols.

Unlike earlier tribal confederations over-running Eurasia, the Mongols were not a Turkish people but came from the far east, from the plains of Mongolia. The lands they dominated were far vaster than those of any nomadic predecessors known to the West. They reigned over the whole steppeland, from China to Eastern Europe. This may have been true of earlier confederations, and it might be only a lack of surviving records that

135

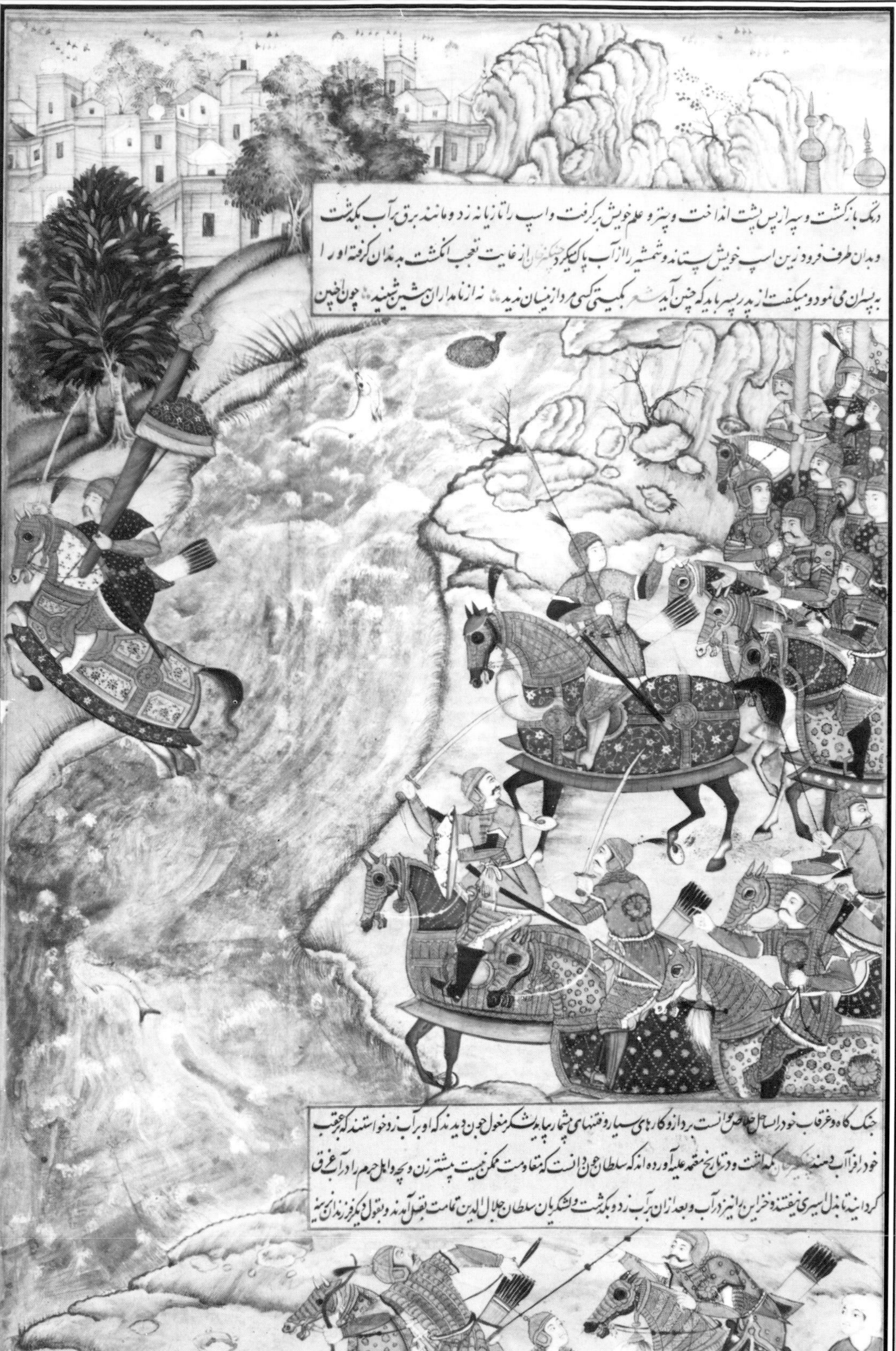

prevent us from making the connection between tribes in European annals and those of a different name in Chinese history: the Huns are believed by some to be of Mongolian origin. But what we do know is that by the beginning of the 13th century, the tribes of Mongolia had been united under the warlord Genghis Khan. Also – as opposed to earlier movements of oriental hordes, spurred onwards by drought, famine or more ferocious rivals – the expanding campaigns of the Mongols seem to have been a self-conscious effort to conquer the known world. Their dominion was imperialistic. To established Eastern and Western empires, however, they were still deadly savages. Frederick II, German Emperor, considered the Tartars *gens barbarae nationis*.

With an Asian domain left secure by Genghis Khan, his successor, Ogedei, over-looked a series of historic campaigns. In 1237, under the command of Batu (the Khan's nephew) and his leading general Subedei, a Mongol horde smashed the kingdoms of the Russians. They advanced during the winter, for in spring when the snows melted, the great rivers were swollen and the country-side a morass. In 1241, the Mongols entered Poland. Near the town of Liegnitz, Duke Henry of Silesia and the Grand Master of the Teutonic Order assembled a major force of Poles and Germans. Western knights, clad in mail, confronted the eastern marauders. At the end of the day, nine sacks of ears, cut off their European opponents, were collected by the victorious Mongols. From there the Mongol army, divided into independent forces, met up in Hungary and devastated the feudal host of King Bela at the battle of Mohi. Within a few days, the Mongols had delivered two catastrophic blows to Western defences. The Emperor Frederick now feared for the security of his own lands and wrote to his

fellow monarchs asking for assistance in a crisis which 'concerns not only the Roman Empire, but all kingdoms of the world that practise Christian worship'. Signs were not encouraging for concerted action against the Mongols. Only a few years earlier, Muslim leaders had sent ambassadors to the West to encourage an alliance between the two religions in order to rid the world of the infidel nomads. While the English king had pondered this request, one of his bishops interrupted, 'Let us leave these dogs – Saracen and pagan – to devour one another. So that when we proceed against those enemies of Christ that remain we will slay them and the whole world will be subject to the one Catholic Europe.' Such an attitude had brought the Mongols to the borders of the German Empire.

In his letter to all Western monarchs, Frederick outlined what little was known of the military qualities of the Mongol enemy. 'They are ready at the nod of their leader to rush into any undertaking. They wear raw hides of oxen and to these are sewn iron plates. Portable boats, also made of hide, enable them to cross over any rivers. From the spoils of conquered Christians, they are providing themselves with fine weapons so that we may be slain by our own arms. They are incomparable archers. The bow is a more familiar weapon to them than to any other people. From their regular use of it, their arms are stronger than other people and they have entirely subdued nations because of this.' The excellent archery and boiled-leather armour of the Mongols was attested by other European observers, including Marco Polo; but it was not only their clouds of arrows that devastated European warriors. Military discipline and strategy was of a very high standard among the Mongols, although it must be remembered that it was only the leading officers and commanders of the horde who were of Mongolian origin. The majority of Mongol warriors who invaded Europe in the 13th century were drawn from Turkish Eurasian tribes that had been absorbed into their confederation: no different to the previous waves of Barbarians.

Western reaction to the Mongols was feeble. Though called on to send their bravest warriors, those monarchs beyond the German Empire saw little advantage in helping their political rivals. Matthew Paris recorded that Frederick's sons did gather together an impressive force and indeed defeated the Mongols on the banks of the river Delpheos, not far from the Danube. But this has not been substantiated, and by the winter of 1241 the Mongols stood poised to invade Germany and Italy. Raiders rode into the Balkans, pursuing the Hungarian King Bela. Venice and Vienna were perilously close to being pulverised by the ingenious siege machines of the Mongols. Then, from the plains of central Asia, hard-riding messengers brought news of the death of the great Khan. Dissension between the leading Mongols made it vital for all contenders to the succession to return eastwards, and the campaign was broken off: miraculous deliverance for the West.

From what evidence we have, the military expertise of the Mongols exceeded that of any previous Eurasian eruption into Europe. The West had

With the fragmentation of Mongol unity, no Eurasian confederation was ever again to sweep into Europe from the steppelands north of the Black Sea. A late 19th century engraving.

never been as close to absolute submission to an eastern steppe confederation as it was during the 13th century. The Huns, Avars and Magyars penetrated further westward and left a greater impact on European culture than the Mongols, but they did not possess the sophisticated administration to turn their campaigns into major conquests. Fortunately for Europe, fragmentation among the Mongol royal families cut short their expansion and they lacked the dynamism to repeat their invasion of 1241. Ancient Scythia now became the western-most province of the Khanate of the Golden Horde. The steppes north of the Black Sea were never again to be a launching pad for any major nomadic incursion into Europe. That said, the terror of the Turks was not at an end. During the 14th, 15th and 16th centuries, Turks of the Ottoman confederation rampaged through Asia Minor, overran the Balkans and terrorised central Europe. With the Turkish capture of Constantinople in 1453, the Byzantines, the last direct inheritors of the Greek and Roman tradition, were swept away. Only the German Holy Roman Empire now remained to protect the West against the Turks. But because the Barbarians were essentially a creation of the Greeks and Romans, the term had lost its meaning with the ending of a Mediterranean Empire. There were no longer any outsiders — northern and eastern wildmen — battering on the frontiers of a Graeco-Latin world. The disappearance of their ancient adversaries meant that the Barbarians also ceased to exist.

Bibliography

THIS IS, OF NECESSITY A SELECT BIBLIOGRAPHY OF
BOTH PRIMARY AND SECONDARY REFERENCES

Primary Sources

ALL THESE TEXTS ARE AVAILABLE IN ENGLISH TRANSLATIONS IN SEVERAL
EDITIONS.

Ammianus Marcellinus, *Roman History:* 4th century account of Barbarian
invasions by a Greek 'officer and gentleman'

Anonymous, *Beowulf:* 8th century Anglo-Saxon epic poem

Anonymous, *The Wanderer* and *The Seafarer:* 10th century Anglo-Saxon
poems

Anonymous, *The Battle of Maldon:* 10th century Anglo-Saxon poetical
account of battle in 991

Caesar, *The Gallic War:* 1st century BC autobiography of campaigns against
Celts and Germans

Constantine Porphyrogenitus, *De Administrando Imperio:* 10th century
compilation of Byzantine history by Emperor Constantine VII

Einhard and Notker the Stammerer, *Lives of Charlemagne:* 9th century
accounts of the Frank Emperor. One by a courtier, the other by a monk
sometime after Charlemagne's death

Fredegar, *The Fourth Book of the Chronicle:* 6th to 8th century Frank history
by several authors

Gregory of Tours, *The History of the Franks:* 6th century chronicle of the
Franks by a Gallo-Roman bishop

Jordanes, *Getica: The Origin and Deeds of the Goths:* 6th century history of
the Goths by an Italian monk

Liutprand of Cremona, *Antapodosis:* 10th century chronicle by an Italian
bishop and ambassador to the German Emperor

Nestor, *The Russian Primary Chronicles:* 9th to 12th century history of
Russia compiled by a 12th century monk

Matthew Paris, *Historia Major:* 13th century English history including
continental affairs compiled by an English monk

140

Velleius Paterculus, *History of Rome:* 1st century history by a Roman army officer

Paul the Deacon, *History of the Lombards:* 8th century chronicle of the Lombards by an Italian monk

Priscus, *Fragments:* 5th century eye-witness accounts by an eastern Roman official

Procopius, *History of the Persian, Vandal, and Goth wars:* 6th century eye-witness accounts by a Greek secretary to Belisarius

Strabo, *Geographica:* 1st century description of all known peoples by a Greek traveller and writer

Tacitus, *The Annals, Histories, and Germania:* 1st century history written by a Roman politician.

Zosimus, *Historia Nova: The Decline of Rome:* 5th century eastern Roman history by a Greek official

Secondary Works

Bachrach, BS, 'Charles Martel, Mounted Shock Combat, The Stirrup, and Feudalism', *Studies in Medieval and Renaissance History*, Vol VII, p49, Lincoln, Nebraska, 1970.

Bachrach, BS, *Merovingian Military Organization 481–751*, Minneapolis, 1972.

Bachrach, BS, *A History of the Alans in the West*, University of Minnesota Press. Minneapolis, 1973.

Bivar, ADH, 'Cavalry Equipment and Tactics on the Euphrates Frontier', *Dumbarton Oaks Papers*, Vol XXVI, p273, Washington, 1972.

Blondal, S and Benedikz, BS, *The Varangians of Byzantium*, Cambridge, 1978.

Boba, I, *Nomads, Northmen and Slavs*, the Hague, 1967.

Brøgger, AW and Shetelig, H, *The Viking Ships*, Oslo, 1951.

Burgess, EM, 'The Mail-Maker's Technique', *Antiquaries Journal*, XXXIII, p48, London, 1953.

Butler, AJ, *The Arab Conquest of Egypt*, Oxford, 1902.

Czarnecki, J, *The Goths in Ancient Poland*, Miami, 1975.

Davidson, HRE, *The Sword in Anglo-Saxon England*, Oxford, 1962.

Davidson, HRE, *The Viking Road to Byzantium*, London, 1976.

Drew, KF (editor), *The Barbarian Invasions*, New York, 1970.

Dunlop, DM, *The History of the Jewish Khazars*, Princeton, 1954.

Foote, P and Wilson, DM, *The Viking Achievement*, London, 1970.

Gimbutas, M, *The Slavs*, London, 1976.

Glob, PV, *The Bog People*, London, 1969.

Goffart, W, *Barbarians and Romans*, Princeton, 1980.

Gordon, CD, *The Age of Attila*, Michigan, 1960.

Hassall, MWC, and Ireland, R (editors), 'De Rebus Bellicis', *BAR International Series*, 63, Oxford, 1979.

Havighurst, AF (editor), *The Pirenne Thesis*, Lexington, 1976.

Hoffmeyer, AB, 'Military Equipment In the Byzantine Manuscript of Scylitzes', *Gladius*, V, Granada, 1966.

Kagan, D (editor), *The End of the Roman Empire*, Lexington, 1978.

Leyser, K, 'The Battle at the Lech', 955, *History*, L, p1, London, 1965.

Maenchen-Helfen, JO, *The World of the Huns*, Los Angeles, 1973.

Macartney, CA, *The Magyars in the Ninth Century*, Cambridge, 1930.

Nicolle, D, 'Early Medieval Islamic Arms and Armour', *Gladius*, tomo especial, Madrid, 1976.

Parry, VJ and Yapp, ME (editors), *War, Technology and Society in the Middle East*, London, 1975.

Paterson, WF, 'The Archers of Islam', *Journal of the Economic and Social History of the Orient*, 9, p69, Leiden, 1966.

Pipes, D, *Slave Soldiers and Islam*, New Haven, 1981.

Rausing, G, *The Bow*, Lund, Sweden, 1967.

Russom, GR, 'A Germanic Concept of Nobility in *The Gift* and *Beowulf*', *Speculum*, LIII, p1, Cambridge, Massachusetts, 1978.

Saunders, JJ, *The History of the Mongol Conquests*, London, 1971.

Setton, KM, 'The Bulgars in the Balkans in the 7th century', *Speculum*, XXV, p502, Cambridge, Massachusetts, 1950.

Sulimirski, T, *The Sarmatians*, London, 1970.

Thompson, EA, *A History of Attila and the Huns*, Oxford, 1948.

Thompson, EA, *The Early Germans*, Oxford, 1965.

Thompson, EA, *The Visigoths in the time of Ulfila*, Oxford, 1966.

Thompson, EA, *Romans and Barbarians*, Wisconsin, 1982.

Todd, M, *The Northern Barbarians BC 100 to AD 300*, London, 1975.

Vasiliev, AA, *The Russian Attack on Constantinople in 860*, Cambridge, Massachusetts, 1946.

Vasiliev, AA, 'The Second Russian Attack on Constantinople', *Dumbarton Oaks Papers*, VI p165, Cambridge, Massachusetts, 1951.

Wallace-Hadrill, JM, *The Barbarian West 400–1000*, London, 1967.

White, L, *Medieval Technology and Social Change*, Oxford, 1962.

ACKNOWLEDGEMENTS

Illustrations by courtesy of following: British Museum, London 6, 15, 22, 54, 56, 57, 58, 59, 60, 61, 74, 81, 85, 87, 89, 94, 103, 122–123, 127, 130, 131: Peter Newark's Historical Pictures, Bath 2, 10, 11, 13, 14, 16, 17, 19, 23, 25, 29, 31, 32 l & r, 34, 35, 36, 37, 38, 41, 42, 46, 47 t & b, 49, 50, 53, 63, 67, 69, 71, 79, 91, 97, 103, 105, 107, 110, 112, 117, 121, 124, 132, 133, 135, 136, 137, 139.

Archaeological Institute of the Czechoslovak Academy of Sciences, Brno 124; Hermitage Museum, Leningrad 16, 17; National Museum of Antiquities, Helsinki 112; Schleswig-Holstein Landesmuseum 115; State Prehistorical Collection, Munich 33, 34, 36, 37, 69, 71.

Index